Wanderlust Within: A Journey to Self-Discovery

Ilise Litwin

Dedication

This book is dedicated to the most important men in my life.

My Dad, Robert Rosenfeld was a man who always instilled in me to reach for my dreams. I loved the way he always told my daughters they could be anything they wanted to be. In that mindset, I have always wanted to write a book. My Dad is no longer with me, but I can still hear his voice saying, "You can be and do anything you want to." Thank you, Dad, for showing me that I am capable and powerful enough to fulfill my dreams.

Darren Litwin is my husband and my best friend. My husband constantly supports me to reach for my goals. I am so lucky and blessed to have him by my side in this Journey called Life. I love you, Darren, More, More, More! Now, let's do this!!!!

CONTENTS

Dedication iii

About the Author xiii

Wide Open Space xiv

Introduction xv

    Lifelong Learning xvi

    Self-Discovery xvi

    Giving Ourselves Power xvii

    Exploring Oneself and Being Self-Aware xvii

    Recognizing Our Advantages and Disadvantages xvii

    Making Our Aspirations and Values Clear xviii

    Establishing the Foundations for Development xviii

Chapter 1 – The Next Phase of My Journey 1

    Exploring the Individual 2

    Group Therapy 3

    The Road to Resilience 3

    Empowering Patients for the Future 4

    The Transition to Motherhood 5

    Self-Reflection and Identity 5

    Discovering My Legacy 6

Virtual Resilience in a Time of Isolation 7

The Impact of Empathy 8

The Birth of a New Idea 9

Defining the Mission 9

A Transformation Beyond Roles 10

Sharing Wisdom and Legacy 10

Chapter 2 – A Million Dreams in Solitude 12

Chapter 3 – Transforming Your Loneliness into Personal Empowerment 23

Chapter 4 – Notes of Strength Amid Chaos 33

1. Reframe Your Thoughts: 39

2. One Task at a Time: 39

3. Speak to the Positive: 39

4. Distractions: 40

5. Mindfulness and Breathing: 40

6. Socialize: 40

7. Acknowledge Successes: 40

8. Self-Care: 41

Chapter 5 – How Music Shapes the Journey Within 43

Chapter 6 – Beyond The Crossroads 53

Work-Life Balance Changes: 55

Hobby and Interest Development:...55

Leisure and Recreation:...56

Holistic Health Practices:...56

Boundaries and Digital Detox:.......................................56

Purpose of the Podcast:..57

A Mosaic of Options:...57

Pieces of a Puzzle:..57

Personalized Rearrangement:..58

Tailored to Your Journey:..58

An Ongoing Investigation:..58

Inspiration from Robert Frost's Poem:...............................58

Standing at the Crossroads:..59

Visualizing Your Divergent Paths:...................................59

Personal Crossroads:...59

The Well-Traveled Road:...60

The Path Less Traveled:..60

Decision-Making Agency:..60

Learning from Crossroads:...60

Moving Forward with Intention:.....................................61

Taking the Road Less Traveled......................................61

The Comfort Zone as a Starting Point:..............................61

Recognizing the Need for Progress:.................................61

The Catalyst for Change:..62

Overcoming Fear of the Unknown:..62

Uncharted Territory:..62

Learning From Hurdles:...62

The Evolutionary Power of Choices:..63

Fostering a Mindset of Potential:...63

Setting Intentional Challenges:..63

Career Choices:..64

Relationship Choices:...64

Personal Development:..64

Lessons Discovered:...65

The Ripple Effect:..65

Your Own Personal Adventure:..65

Visualization Exercise..65

Decision-Making and Coping Skills...67

Chapter 7 – In the Mirror of Self-Reflection..................................73

Anxiety in the Spotlight..73

A Personal Exploration of Anxiety's Evolution.............................74

The Waves of Change...76

Demystifying Anxiety...78

The Pandemic as a Precipitating Factor..80

Tools and Resources for Coping...82

Self-Awareness Mirror Exercise 84

Taking Control of Your Mental Health.................................85

Novel Approaches to Anxiety 87

Chapter 8 – The Inner Superpower 91

Acknowledgment and Dedication 91

Being Your Own Superhero 93

Superhero Coping Skills...94

Taking Risks and Overcoming Anxiety 97

□   Fear of Failure:...99

□   Perfectionism: 99

□   Overestimation of Risk: 99

□   Comfort in the Familiar: 100

□   Mindful Self-Reflection:..100

□   Redefining Failure: 100

□   Gradual Exposure: 100

□   Setting Realistic Goals:..101

□   Cultivating a Growth Mindset: 101

Embrace the Hero Within...101

□   Facing the Fear of Another Failed Marriage: 102

□   Experiencing a Panic Attack:......................................103

□   Two Choices: Self-Sabotage or Seeking Help:..........104

□   Therapeutic Intervention:..104

☐   The Result: A Resilient 16-Year Marriage: 105

Empowering Others: Inspiring Positive Change 106

Supporting Others and Seeking Help 107

Identifying Symptoms of Panic Attacks...................................109

Chapter 9 - Reinvent Your Brave Soul 111

Embracing the Reality of Life's Uncertainties 111

Reinventing Yourself: What Does It Mean? 111

Evolving Nature of Personal Identity and Goals....................113

Concrete Steps to Reinvention: 114

A.   Reflecting on One's Own Goals and Desires: 114

B.   Making a Wish List to Grow Both Professionally and
Personally: 115

C.   Determining Neglected Objectives and Proactively Pursuing
Them: 115

Overcoming Resistance and Self-Doubt: 116

A.   Identifying Self-doubt and Reluctance to Change:..........116

B.   Promoting Taking Chances and Venturing Beyond Your
Comfort Zones:..117

C.   Stressing the Value of Endurance and Patience in the Process
of Reinvention: 117

Organic Reinvention: Allowing Change to Happen 118

A.   Exploring How Life Experiences Can Naturally Lead to
Reinvention:...118

B.   Organic Reinvention During The Pandemic.....................118

C.   Accepting Unforeseen Chances for Personal Development and Exploration:...120

Sharing and Connecting Through Reinvention.....................121

A.   Highlighting the Therapeutic Benefits of Sharing Personal Experiences..121

B.   Engage and Share Your Own Reinvention Journeys.......121

Reflecting on the Transformative Power of Reinvention......123

Chapter 10 – The Evolution Diaries......................................125

Symbolism of Goddesses and Gods.....................................125

Empowerment in the Midst of Challenging Times 125

Evolution Through Ages 127

☐ 20s: Uninhibited Discovery and Ambitious Beginnings......127

☐ 30s: Establishing Roots, Building a Career, and Entering Parenthood 127

☐ 40s: Getting to Know Oneself and Questioning Life's Deeper Meaning 128

☐ 50s: Finding Enlightenment, Acknowledging Constant Change, and Blossoming 129

☐ Reflection on the Unique Evolution of Each Stage 129

Embracing Change and Growth 130

☐ Shifting Perspective on Oneself:...131

☐ Modifying Self-Talk and Permitting Positive Influences: ...131

□   Assessing and Modifying Relationships:..............................132

□   The Magnificence of Being Wholly Oneself:......................132

Navigating the Uncertainties...132

□   Recognizing the Challenges and Adapting to a Changing World: 133

□   Finding Growth and Strength in the Face of Adversity:.......134

□   Acknowledging Personal Loss and Embracing Life's Uncertainties:...134

Incorporating Quotes that Resonate with the Theme:............135

□   Sharing Personal Insights and Reflections:.........................135

Empowering Others: Inspiring Positive Change.....................136

□   Encouraging Self-Reflection and Embracing Personal Growth: 137

Highlighting the Importance of Moving Forward During Challenging Times: 137

Motivating Everyday Objectives for the Spirit, Body, and Mind: 137

Stressing the Need for Emotional Health and Self-Care:.......138

Practicing Mindfulness and Gratitude in Everyday Life:.......138

Reflecting on the Transformative Power of Challenging Experiences: 138

Encouraging Readers to Embrace the Journey to Their Best Selves: 138

Exploring the Wide Open Spaces in One's World:.............139

Chapter 11 – The Quest Within.............140

Explore Your Own Paths and Aspirations 140

Understanding Roadblocks 141

    I.   Exploring The Concept of Roadblocks in Life's Journey....141

    II.   Tangible and Intangible Roadblocks 141

Coping with Stress and Uncertainty.............143

    I.   Personal Shield: The Coping Strategy 143

    II.   Implementing Self-care Practices 144

Exploring Inner Strength.............146

    ☐   Significance of Inner Strength and Resilience.............146

Nurturing The Self 147

    ☐   Prioritize Self-Care and Introspection 147

Embracing Possibilities 148

Conclusion.............150

Take On Obstacles With Bravery and Hope 151

Resilience In Handling The Ups And Downs Of Life 151

Encouraging Ongoing Self-Reflection and Growth 152

Resources For Further Exploration And Support.............153

About the Author

Ilise Litwin, aka The Fiery Redhead, has a Bachelor of Science in Recreation from the University of Florida. Go Gators! Ilise has worked in the mental health field in hospital Mental Health Units and Outpatient programs. Ilise's expertise is in Geriatrics, Pediatrics/Adolescents, Dual Diagnosis, Cancer Wellness, and Alcohol and Drug Rehabilitation. As a Therapeutic Recreational Specialist, Ilise has worked with clients on their coping mechanisms, healthy lifestyle habits, and decreased anxiety and helped her clients identify ways to increase their moods and adapt to life's challenges. Following the mass High School Shooting, Ilise began to see an extreme mental health crisis in her community. A few years later, Covid hit, and Ilise saw a huge need to share her professional knowledge and her life experiences with an audience. Ilise has successfully published over 150 Episodes of her Podcast and has reached audiences all over the world. Her main goal is to connect with her listeners and readers on a personal level. Bringing to the forefront that everyone struggles, and there are many ways to initiate a new level of self-awareness and care for ourselves.

Wide Open Space

In the heart of boundless lands,
Where the sky kisses the earth,
She stands—a flame against the canvas,
A wild spirit, unbridled by time.

Her hair, a cascade of copper,
Touched by sun and wind,
Echoes the hues of rolling hills,
And the secrets whispered by ancient trees.

Her eyes, like forgotten constellations,
Hold stories of wanderlust and wonder,
Of dreams woven into the fabric of clouds,
And the promise of uncharted paths.

In this wilderness, she finds solace,
A sanctuary where echoes fade,
And the silence sings its sweet refrain:
"Embrace the open spaces within.

Introduction

Greetings from the beginning of a new chapter in your life, my dear friends. This is a journey full of self-love, personal development, and realizing your limitless potential. Let's follow this transforming route with open minds and hearts, prepared to accept the delicate, wonderful process of becoming who we truly are.

Developing oneself mentally, spiritually, and physically is all part of the holistic process of personal development. It is about realizing our innate talents and the areas in which we desire to grow and then fearlessly embarking on a journey of self-awareness and development. Everybody has a different journey, one that is molded by their own experiences, goals, and challenges overcome.

While goal-setting and achievement play a part, it's not the only aspect of it. It's about developing the ability to live intentionally and make decisions that are in line with our core beliefs and goals. It's about developing compassion, empathy, and resilience—not only for other people but also for ourselves.

We'll explore every area of personal development, from developing a growth mindset and improving emotional intelligence to promoting physical and spiritual well-being. In order to strengthen our connections with one another and with ourselves, this path encourages us to view vulnerability as a strength.

We'll learn together that personal growth is a continuous process of becoming. It challenges us to maintain our curiosity, openness, and dedication to the never-ending quest for knowledge and development.

It pushes us to face our anxieties, leave our comfort zones, and accept the ambiguity and transience that characterize the human experience.

Lifelong Learning

A lifetime of learning is the foundation of ongoing development. This involves adopting an attitude of openness and curiosity as well as learning new abilities and information. It entails having an inquisitive mindset, always seeking clarification, and approaching life with awe. My dear friends, we recognize that there is always more to learn about the world we live in and, most significantly, about ourselves when we make the commitment to be lifelong learners. My connection with the world and with myself has changed as a result of this method, which views every moment as a chance for growth and learning.

Self-Discovery

The process of self-discovery is one that never really ends. To find our true selves, we must peel back the layers of our experiences, values, and beliefs. This process might be difficult; we might have to face aspects of ourselves that we've repressed or denied. However, it is during this investigation that we discover our actual power and calling. I've discovered that the more I understand about who I am, the more I acknowledge how much I don't know. And we experience the deepest personal development and metamorphosis on this path, my dear friends.

Giving Ourselves Power

By making the commitment to keep growing, we give ourselves more power. We grow adaptive, able to ride the waves of change with power and grace. This empowerment is about realizing our ability to live a purposeful and happy life, not merely about conquering problems. As we go on this path of self-improvement, new avenues become accessible to us that we never would have thought.

Exploring Oneself and Being Self-Aware

The first step in the journey is reflection, a close examination of our innermost selves. This process is about comprehending our inner selves, not just accepting where we are right now. It entails analyzing our values, beliefs, anxieties, and dreams. We acquire the self-awareness required to identify the areas of our lives that most require change through introspection. My friends, this self-awareness is a really useful skill. It serves as a compass, assisting us in handling the challenges of personal development and making sure we stay loyal to our most genuine selves.

Recognizing Our Advantages and Disadvantages

Recognizing our strengths and shortcomings is a crucial step in laying the foundation for change. This is an honest evaluation stage rather than one that involves self-criticism or judgment. Acknowledging our strengths enables us to capitalize on them and employ them as pillars of support to help us through our path. Having an understanding of our flaws, however, is just as crucial. It assists us in identifying our areas of growth, the obstacles we must face, and the potential need for support or the acquisition of new abilities. Recall that admitting our shortcomings is a sign of strength and the first step toward development and bettering ourselves.

Making Our Aspirations and Values Clear

Our values form the cornerstone of our lives, directing our choices, forming our actions, and impacting our interpersonal interactions. By making our values clear, we can better understand what is important to us and make sure that our transformational path is in line with our core values. In addition, figuring out our goals provides us with a direction and a goal to work toward. Whether these goals are spiritual, professional, or personal, they are like lights in the darkness that inspire us and give our path direction and meaning.

Establishing the Foundations for Development

When we practice introspection, reflect on our strengths and limitations, and define our values and goals, we create the groundwork for meaningful growth and fulfillment. This foundation serves as more than just a place to start; it is a basis that keeps us going as we go. It allows us to go on with resilience and confidence since it is based on self-knowledge, self-acceptance, and self-respect.

Let's take the lessons we've learned here with us as we continue on our trip. Let's embrace self-reflection and self-awareness, realizing how crucial it is to comprehend who we are on a deeper level. Let us make sure that our route is in line with our most profound beliefs and ambitions by making our values and aspirations clear.

Above all, though, let's not forget that developing oneself is about loving the journey rather than merely arriving at a goal. It's about having the guts to take chances, the fortitude to get beyond setbacks, and the will to improve upon ourselves. Thus, let's move on with open minds and hearts, prepared to welcome the opportunities that lie ahead.

Chapter 1 – The Next Phase of My Journey

In a world where the power of words can shape destinies and transform lives, I once shied away from speaking about myself. But, I've come to realize the profound importance of sharing one's professional journey. Let me take you on a captivating journey through my career, a voyage that began at the esteemed University of Florida, where I earned my Bachelor of Science Degree. As a Certified Therapeutic Recreational Specialist (CTRS), I ventured into a realm that traversed the boundaries of conventional healthcare. My journey has taken me through a variety of settings, including Psychiatric Hospitals, Outpatient Programs, and Outpatient Rehabilitation Facilities, each offering a unique platform for me to apply my skills and expertise.

My voyage didn't merely traverse the horizons of various healthcare settings; it delved deep into the lives of a multitude of individuals. From the innocence of Pediatrics and Adolescents to the complexities of Mental Health Diagnoses and Dual Diagnosis Disorders, my experiences ran the gamut. I've ventured into the world of addiction, providing solace to those battling Chemical Dependency and offering support to individuals grappling with the challenges of Eating Disorders. My compass pointed me toward the realm of Cancer Wellness, where resilience and hope become the bedrock of recovery. The wisdom of age beckoned me, leading me to care for Geriatric Patients, where compassion and understanding were my guiding stars. Alzheimer's and Memory Disorders, domains where memories fade but hearts retain their essence, also found their place in my journey. Additionally, I extended my hands to those who often go unnoticed, the Homeless Population, within the compassionate embrace of a hospital setting.

In every step, I've found fulfillment and a profound sense of purpose, knowing that I could impact the lives of individuals in countless ways.

As a dedicated healthcare professional, my journey in aiding individuals on their path to recovery has been an incredibly fulfilling one. Each step has been marked by personal interactions that have shaped the way I approach my role as a therapist.

Exploring the Individual

My excursion began with the initial one-on-one meetings with each patient. In these sessions, I have the privilege of listening to their unique stories, fears, and aspirations. These moments were not just about gathering medical data but understanding the individuals behind the diagnoses. Every person had their own set of challenges and their personal objectives for their stay at the hospital or in the outpatient program.

This individualized approach allowed me to connect with them on a human level, gaining insight into their motivations, fears, and hopes. It was through these conversations that I realized the true essence of my work lay in understanding the patient as a whole, not just as a list of symptoms or a medical case.

Group Therapy

The therapeutic groups I conducted with about 10-15 patients at a time were an integral part of our recovery program. These sessions became a platform for patients to share their thoughts and experiences, fostering a sense of community and solidarity. By discussing topics like coping mechanisms for dealing with anxiety, depression, mood swings, and illness, we encouraged open and honest conversations that were both therapeutic and empowering.

The power of the group dynamic cannot be underestimated. Patients discovered that they were not alone in their struggles, and this realization was a cornerstone in their journey to recovery. Through these group discussions, they learned from one another, and many found solace in knowing that there were others who could relate to their challenges.

The Road to Resilience

One of the fundamental principles I emphasized throughout the therapy groups was the importance of incorporating leisure as a coping mechanism. The concept of leisure as therapy might seem unusual at first, but it holds a wealth of benefits for patients. By engaging in enjoyable and fulfilling activities, patients could find an escape from their worries, build their self-esteem, and regain a sense of control over their lives.

I often shared stories of patients who had successfully integrated leisure activities into their daily routines and how they had transformed their lives. From painting and reading to gardening and even taking up new hobbies, these leisure pursuits became an essential part of the recovery process.

Empowering Patients for the Future

Lastly, it was not enough to focus on their hospital or outpatient stay alone. We emphasized the need to formulate a plan for life after discharge. This transition could be daunting, but it was also an opportunity for patients to put into practice the coping mechanisms they had learned during their stay. We worked together to establish realistic, achievable goals, ensuring that the path forward was clear and supported.

The role of a therapist allowed me to witness the human spirit's resilience in action. It was not just a job; it was a calling. The personal connections forged during therapy sessions were deeply meaningful, as I helped individuals uncover their inner strengths and learn to cope with their struggles. The sense of satisfaction that arose from watching my patients regain control over their lives was immeasurable.

As I immersed myself in the world of therapeutic engagement and patient care, life had an unexpected turn in store for me. The prospect of motherhood once again brought significant change into my life. Unlike my first pregnancy, this time, it was a challenging and often tumultuous experience. As a result, I had to make the difficult decision to temporarily put my profession on the back burner. It was a turning point that brought about a period of self-reflection and transformation.

The Transition to Motherhood

During my second pregnancy, I found myself in the midst of a medical rollercoaster. The complications and discomfort I faced were unlike anything I had encountered before. The demands of pregnancy, coupled with the responsibility of caring for my older daughter, made it clear that I needed to temporarily step back from my career.

The decision to become a stay-at-home mom to my two daughters was a turning point. It was a decision that I embraced with open arms. The days were filled with diaper changes, feeding schedules, and lullabies. There was something profoundly satisfying about this part of my life, a feeling of connection and fulfillment I couldn't have anticipated. I recognized that my daughters wouldn't be little girls forever, and I wanted to be present and cherish every moment.

Self-Reflection and Identity

Yet, as my daughters grew, so did the questions and doubts within me. I couldn't help but wonder about my own personal evolution. My life, like that of many stay-at-home mothers, seemed to revolve around the domestic sphere and the needs of my children. This period of introspection brought to light the questions that many parents eventually confront: What happens to a stay-at-home mom when her kids grow older and become more independent?

The turning point came one day when I found myself sitting on the couch, watching my kids being busy on their cell phones. It was a quiet moment when the house seemed to echo with a profound question: "Is this what the rest of my life will look like? Making no impact on the world. What would my legacy be?"

Throughout my life, I have been driven by a deep desire to make a positive impact on the world. The roles I embraced - as a therapist, a mother, and a support system for those in need - were all connected by a common thread: the yearning to help and uplift others. However, there was a lingering sense that my purpose had not yet fully revealed itself.

It was during a time of introspection, in the quiet solitude of my backyard, that I began to question my path and consider what more I could offer to the world. It was as if I were listening for a call, a signal that would illuminate my true purpose and guide me in a new direction.

These questions weighed heavily on my mind. I grappled with the idea that my life might be forever bound to the role of a mother and homemaker. And yet, as time passed, I arrived at a crucial realization: Yes, this is what my life would look like from now on, but it didn't mean it couldn't evolve and take on new dimensions.

Discovering My Legacy

This was the moment for me to rediscover my actual purpose! During this moment of self-discovery and self-acceptance, I went on a quest to reclaim my identity as a committed mother as well as a passionate professional. I still wanted to make a positive difference in the world, and I knew I could find a way to combine my obligations at home with a feeling of purpose outside my family.

My journey as a therapist, though momentarily put on hold, was not forgotten. I began to explore opportunities to engage in my profession while still being there for my little girls.

Then, in December of 2019, it was as if the universe responded with a call of its own. A global pandemic began to grip the world, changing the course of our lives and reshaping our understanding of what it meant to be human. The world was in lockdown, and our homes became our sanctuaries.

The world changed rapidly, and it was during this extraordinary time that the power of human resilience became ever more evident. In a world of lockdowns, quarantines, and uncertainty, new coping mechanisms emerged, and the virtual realm became the primary means of connecting with others.

During these challenging times, a powerful force within me was awakened. As the pandemic engulfed us, the need for support and solace surged. People were grappling with the immense weight of COVID-19, the pain of loss, the relentless anxiety, the suffocating grip of depression, the gnawing loneliness, and the chaos of a world in disarray.

It was in this moment of crisis that I felt a profound calling, as if a divine purpose had finally been revealed to me. I continued to give therapy, even in the midst of a global pandemic. Friends, family, and acquaintances reached out, seeking guidance, comfort, or simply someone to listen to and empathize with their struggles.

Virtual Resilience in a Time of Isolation

With the onset of the pandemic, people began to experience a myriad of challenges – the fear of the virus, the sorrow of loss, anxiety, depression, loneliness, the absence of social interactions, and the chaos that surrounded us. Like many, I found myself navigating these turbulent waters, and the solace of self-reflection became a part of my daily routine.

I spent countless hours alone, particularly in my backyard, pondering the state of the world and the multitude of emotions it stirred within me. Despite the isolation, I was never truly alone. I continued to be a therapist, albeit in a new and evolving way. Friends, family, and acquaintances reached out to me, seeking help, advice, or simply an empathetic ear to listen to their struggles. This unexpected role as a source of support gave me a sense of accomplishment and reassurance that I was making a difference in a world that had become increasingly uncertain.

The Impact of Empathy

One of the most poignant aspects of this period was hearing how my voice and the way I painted a picture of good health and positivity had a profound impact on those I supported. The reassurance I provided, the strategies I shared, and the empathetic conversations that flowed were, in a sense, a lifeline for those grappling with the chaos and uncertainty that the pandemic had unleashed.

This experience taught me that the power of therapy extends far beyond the confines of a clinical setting. It reaffirmed my belief in the resilience of the human spirit, even in the face of adversity. It also underscored the importance of empathy and the art of listening, showing that meaningful connections could be forged even in times of physical separation.

My life experiences had prepared me for this key moment when my skills as a therapist met my intrinsic desire to make a difference in the lives of others. The pandemic confirmed my confidence in the powerful influence of empathy and the human potential to find resilience even in the most difficult of circumstances.

The Birth of a New Idea

As the world grappled with the pandemic, I felt a calling to redefine my role and my contributions. The seeds of reinvention were planted, and I began to ponder how I could harness my unique blend of skills, experiences, and therapeutic background to create something meaningful. This idea led me to a path I had explored during my college days – journalism.

I decided to merge my therapeutic knowledge with my journalism experience to create a platform that could reach a global audience. The concept of a Podcast and Blog resonated with me. Through this medium, I could share my voice, wisdom, and personal and professional experiences with people all over the world.

Defining the Mission

Before launching my Podcast and Blog, I needed to define my mission and choose a title that encapsulated my vision. My love for nature and the idea of filling the empty spaces within ourselves with positive and healthy coping mechanisms served as my inspiration. Thus, "Wide Open Spaces with Ilise" was born. It was a title that encapsulated the journey of self-discovery and healing, inviting others to explore their own wide open spaces.

Starting this new venture was a step into the unknown. I had no idea where this voyage would lead me, but I was determined to make the most of it. My Podcast and Blog got traction as a result of my devotion and hard work, and I was able to reach a global audience. After 130 episodes, it was clear that I had forged a new route for myself.

A Transformation Beyond Roles

The reinvention of my professional life had a profound impact on my identity. I was no longer just a housewife or a stay-at-home mom. I had transitioned into a role that allowed me to reach and inspire people on a global scale. It was a powerful testament to the idea that even in the darkest times, we have the potential to reshape our lives and make a lasting impact.

My mission was clear – I wanted to convey to my readers and listeners that everyone has the capacity to revamp their lives, discover their strengths, and reinvent their daily existence. The old adage, "You can't teach an old dog new tricks," took on new meaning as I delved deep into my own transformation and found a way to make my life more meaningful and productive and to leave a legacy behind.

Sharing Wisdom and Legacy

The most gratifying aspect of this journey has been the connection I've established with my audience. To hear from a listener, sharing how I have positively impacted their life, is an indescribable feeling. It's a reaffirmation that my goal has been accomplished, and I have made a difference in someone's life.

Looking ahead, the next phase of my career involves sharing my words of wisdom, life experiences, and professional expertise through a series of books inspired by my Podcast, "Wide Open Spaces with Ilise." I invite you to join me on this journey into the future. Let's go forward together, exploring the endless possibilities that life has to offer.

While my Podcast has connected me with listeners from around the world, there are those who may not be regular podcast consumers or who prefer the immersive experience of a book. Translating my content into written form enables me to extend my reach and connect with readers in a way that resonates with them. It broadens the scope of my mission, allowing me to make a meaningful impact on even more lives. I am confident that the rewards will far outweigh the challenges. The opportunity to impact lives on a broader scale and to create a legacy that endures is a goal that drives me forward.

Chapter 2 – A Million Dreams in Solitude

Welcome to a journey into the complexities of human experience, where we will explore the vast differences between loneliness and solitude. Loneliness arises as a heartbreaking battle in the fabric of social solitude, distinguished by a craving for meaningful relationships and the weight of emotional suffering. We automatically avoid it, painfully aware of its detrimental influence on our well-being.

Enter solitude, on the other hand—an intentional and enthusiastic embracing of being alone. Consider it a sanctuary where inner awareness reigns supreme, concentrating on personal needs and providing a blank canvas for self-reflection. In contrast to its melancholy counterpart, solitude creates a distinct landscape—one that conjures sentiments of serenity and freedom. This investigation invites us to intentionally open the door to times of contemplation and self-discovery, rejecting the historical myths that have linked solitude to negativity.

In this chapter, I opted for an exploration of solitude and loneliness since it is profoundly entrenched in my observations and reflections. Within the confines of my personal experiences, I distinguish between loneliness—a gloomy state—and solitude—a road to calm and heightened inner awareness. The decision to investigate such a complex subject derives from a conscious contemplation of my own life.

This decision to dig into the subtle worlds of solitude and loneliness is a chosen trip guided by the very heart of my personal experiences and introspections. I am motivated to explore the layers of significance that lie inside the fabric of my own life as I traverse the unfamiliar region of these complicated emotions.

The idea for this investigation stems from a deep desire to comprehend and describe the differences that separate solitude from loneliness. These phrases, which are frequently used interchangeably, contain unique emotional landscapes, and I want to build a better understanding via my personal interactions with both.

I hope to illuminate the personal experiences that have affected my perspective of solitude and loneliness by constructing this narrative. Each reflection adds to my increasing comprehension of these complex states of being.

It is an acknowledgment that, in order to really examine and explain the depths of loneliness and solitude, one must first confront the reflections of these feelings within one's own psyche.

In a society where cultural standards frequently push for the avoidance of solitude, I find myself swimming upstream. I've discovered great significance in seemingly commonplace moments of solitude woven throughout the experiences of my daily existence. I narrate the discovery of good qualities inside solitude via the introspective lens of my own voyage.

Sigmund Freud, a pioneering figure in the field of psychology, explored the intricate relationship between solitude and anxiety, particularly in the context of childhood development. Freud's observations and theories, while influential, have been subject to various interpretations and critiques over time.

Freud posited that moments of solitude, especially during the formative years of childhood, could give rise to feelings of anxiety. His psychoanalytic perspective suggested that when children are left alone, they may confront unfiltered and sometimes unsettling thoughts and emotions. The absence of external stimuli or guidance during these solitary moments might expose the child to the depths of their subconscious, where unresolved conflicts, fears, or repressed desires could surface.

According to Freud, the experience of being alone could become a breeding ground for the emergence of these unconscious elements, contributing to a heightened state of anxiety. The lack of external structures or support systems during solitude, in Freudian terms, could lead to a sense of vulnerability and the potential for internal psychological conflict.

It's important to note that Freud's theories on this matter were formulated within the cultural and historical context of his time, and subsequent advancements in psychology have provided more nuanced perspectives on the relationship between solitude and anxiety. While Freud's ideas contributed significantly to the understanding of the human psyche, contemporary psychology recognizes that the impact of solitude varies widely among individuals and is influenced by numerous factors, including personality, life experiences, and coping mechanisms.

I encourage you to join me in examining the preconceptions

surrounding solitude as I negotiate these historical shadows. Through the introspective prism of my own journey, I hope to shed light on the underlying characteristics that solitude may foster—qualities that have been veiled by historical fallacies and psychological correlations.

Over the years, there has been a transformative evolution in the perception of solitude. Contemporary understanding now distinguishes solitude from its historical conflation with loneliness, illuminating the nuanced dimensions that define this state of being. In light of this evolved perspective, solitude is no longer solely viewed through the lens of negativity; rather, it emerges as a realm that holds the potential for freedom and peace.

The recognition of solitude as distinct from loneliness signifies a paradigm shift, one that acknowledges the inherent value within moments of aloneness. Contrary to the historical narratives that cast solitude as an unwelcome companion, contemporary insights highlight its capacity to offer a respite from the cacophony of external influences. This shift is not merely a semantic distinction but a fundamental reevaluation of the qualities encapsulated within the solitude experience.

In this revised understanding, solitude emerges as a space for personal liberation—a respite from the demands of social interconnectedness. It provides an opportunity for introspection, self-discovery, and the cultivation of inner peace. By disentangling solitude from the historical shackles that bound it to anxiety or inconvenience, we open the door to a more profound appreciation of its positive attributes.

The blank space of loneliness emerged as a huge region for investigation in the aftermath of the lockdown, as the external world came to a halt. The usual patterns that had previously ruled my days had been interrupted, presenting me with a choice: reject the silence or accept it as an opportunity for personal growth. Choosing the latter, I entered the unexplored land of solitude with the purposeful aim of learning its intricacies.

The peace and quiet of my home, which was formerly neglected in the rush and bustle of pre-lockdown life, became a haven for contemplation. The lack of external noise allowed the symphony of my own thoughts to take center stage. My living space's walls, which were once only limits, became witnesses to my inner journey, absorbing the echoes of introspection and self-reflection.

The initial discomfort that came with solitude was real. The abrupt halt of continual external stimulation required addressing ideas and feelings that had long been muffled by the cacophony of daily existence. However, as I leaned into the suffering, I discovered inside myself a reserve of power and perseverance. The loneliness turned out to be a teacher, taking me through the uncharted territory of my own thoughts and emotions.

I began to integrate purposeful times of solitude into my daily routine after establishing a deliberate rhythm inside the silence. This deliberate technique enabled me to peel back the layers of my identity, revealing aspects of myself that the constant demands of a fast-paced society had concealed. In this alone, I discovered long-forgotten passions, cultivated latent creativity, and explored aspects of my personality that had long remained dormant.

This newfound appreciation for solitude became a catalyst for my own broader self-discovery and personal growth. Encouraged by the positive impact of my solitary creative pursuits, I began to integrate intentional moments of aloneness into my routine. This deliberate choice to embrace solitude as a source of inspiration and self-reflection marked a pivotal shift in my mindset.

I found solace in the sanctuary of my backyard, a space that had transformed into a haven for introspection and creativity. The tranquility of nature and the absence of external distractions allowed me to dig deeper into my thoughts and emotions, fostering a heightened sense of mindfulness. I realized that, within this cocoon of solitude, I not only rekindled the joyous activities of my childhood, which were dancing and singing but also unearthed a reservoir of untapped creativity.

The process of engaging with my creative side in solitude became a form of self-expression and a means of connecting with the essence of who I am. It was as if the act of being alone provided the necessary breathing space for my authentic self to emerge, unencumbered by societal expectations or external influences.

In this personal metamorphosis, I recognized the symbiotic relationship between solitude, creativity, and personal well-being. The intentional embrace of solitude as a tool for self-discovery became a transformative practice that rippled into other aspects of my life. I found that the clarity gained in moments of solitude enhanced my decision-making, problem-solving abilities, and overall resilience in the face of life's challenges.

In the midst of the lockdown, another fortuitous chance arose—the birth of my podcast. The introspective journey sparked by the pandemic conditions encouraged me to share my ideas and experiences with a larger audience. Recognizing the transforming gift of self-discovery during difficult times, I set out on a journey to investigate the stories of perseverance, development, and personal evolution that frequently arise in the face of adversity.

This journey of self-discovery through solitude profoundly influenced my perspective, both personally and professionally. It instilled in me a profound respect for the power of intentional aloneness and the myriad opportunities it offered for growth and self-realization.

The pain eventually converted into a sense of release as the days progressed into weeks and months. Once seen as an unfamiliar companion, solitude evolved into an ally in the quest for self-discovery. Rather than repeating the unfamiliarity of self-reflection, the quiet echoed with the sincerity of my inner voice.

The program evolved into a forum for exploring the many facets of solitude and its potential for good development. Each episode attempted to unearth the experiences of those who, like me, had navigated the challenges of solitude and emerged with fresh understanding. It evolved into a digital sanctuary where listeners could find consolation, inspiration, and practical advice on how to use solitude for personal development.

Guests from many walks of life shared their stories, adding to a rich tapestry of anecdotes that emphasized common aspects of the human experience. The podcast became a mosaic of varied viewpoints on the good elements of being alone, from artists finding inspiration in solitude to businesses using times of alone for strategic thinking.

Recognizing the pandemic's obstacles, the podcast acted as a beacon of hope—a reminder that even in times of uncertainty, there is potential for self-discovery and progress. The transformational power of solitude, which I had discovered on my personal path, struck a chord with a worldwide audience struggling with the deep changes brought about by the pandemic.

As the episodes progressed, it became evident that the podcast had outgrown its original goal. It had blossomed into a community, a digital space where people from all over the world could interact over shared experiences. Listeners contacted out, thanking me for reassuring them that they were not alone in their contemplative travels.

In negotiating the pandemic's hurdles, the podcast became more than simply a creative outlet but also a monument to the human spirit's resiliency. It demonstrated people's ability to find courage, purpose, and a feeling of belonging even in the face of extraordinary adversity.

The transformative gift of self-discovery, catalyzed by the circumstances of the pandemic, had not only reshaped my personal narrative but had also rippled outwards, touching the lives of those who tuned in. It became a reminder that within the quietude of solitude, there exists not only personal growth but also the potential to inspire and connect with a broader community—one that, despite physical distances, shares in the collective journey of self-discovery and resilience.

I implore you, my readers, to accept the energizing embrace of solitude. As I recount my personal path of self-discovery during the lockdown, I am struck by the transforming potential that solitude can have in our lives. It's an invitation to transform our perception of solitude from one of discomfort to one of personal growth, creativity, and profound reflection.

To begin this journey, I give practical guidance, realizing that the thought of solitude might be intimidating, especially for individuals who are not used to spending lengthy periods of time alone. Begin with short periods, enabling yourself to adjust gradually. Set out a few minutes each day to be alone with your thoughts, free of interruptions. This might be as easy as taking a leisurely stroll in a local park, sitting in a quiet room, or relaxing in your favorite snug nook.

As you let go of these brief times, pay attention to the ideas and sensations that occur. Accept the discomfort because it has the opportunity for self-discovery. Consider doing anything that makes you happy during these times, whether it's reading, writing, or simply admiring the beauty of nature.

Small rituals might be incorporated into your isolation practice. Consider beginning and ending each session with a moment of mindfulness or deep breathing. These routines may act as anchors, bringing you back to the present moment and making your experience more purposeful.

In the symphony of solitude, where the echoes of inspiring quotes resonate, I find solace in the wisdom encapsulated by Naomi Judd's profound words: *"Solitude is creativity's best friend, and solitude is refreshment for our souls."* These words act as a beacon, reinforcing the transformational effect of isolation on our creative essence and inner well-being. As I think on my own path, these thoughts become more than just words; they are a live witness to the transformative power of purposeful moments spent in silent contemplation.

Deepak Chopra's insight adds yet another layer to this understanding: *"To make the right choice in life, you have to get in touch with your soul. To do this, you need to experience solitude, which most people are afraid of."*

Dear readers, I want to urge you to appreciate the beauty of your own company in your search for real happiness. The richness of our inner worlds sometimes goes unrecognized in the frenzy of daily living. As a result, I encourage you to halt deliberately, carve out periods of solitude, and delve into the depths of your thoughts and emotions. The keys to your real pleasure may be discovered in these peaceful moments.

As a call to action, I encourage you to visit a neighboring park, a beautiful lakeside, or the peaceful comfort of your own garden. Discover the delight of solitude in these vast expanses. Feel the mild air, hear the rustle of leaves, and let the calm of the surroundings take you into a quiet area of thought.

As a companion on your journey, I advise you to listen to "A Million Dreams," a rendition by the artist P!NK from the Broadway show the Greatest Showman. Find inspiration for your own hopes and aspirations in its expressive words and upbeat music. Allow the music to serve as a soundtrack to your periods of isolation, a song that resonates with the boundless possibilities that might emerge when you give yourself the gift of contemplation.

As we stride forward on the path of self-discovery, let us bear the profound wisdom gleaned from this exploration as a guiding light. It is crucial to acknowledge the challenges posed by loneliness and understand the weight it carries on our emotional landscape. Loneliness, often viewed through a lens of somber isolation, demands our compassionate recognition. It is a universal human experience that has the potential to shape our perceptions and responses to solitude.

Let us lend a loving hand to individuals who may be traveling the maze of loneliness as we take this insight forward. By acknowledging and understanding their problems, we help to build a more compassionate world—one in which solitude is not only tolerated but cherished for its ability to generate growth, resilience, and a greater connection with ourselves and others.

May we find peace in the constant struggle of solitude and loneliness, acknowledging that both are essential components of the human experience. Through this insight, we may build a more compassionate and nuanced attitude to isolation, paving the way for a future in which people can negotiate their periods of solitude with grace, resilience, and a profound feeling of connection.

Chapter 3 – Transforming Your Loneliness into Personal Empowerment

I've frequently found myself negotiating tough problems, seeking inspiration, and looking for that vital fuel that drives me toward my objectives. It's in these moments that I've come to realize how powerful being a motivational speaker can be. They have the capacity to reawaken the dormant flame inside others, encouraging them to overcome constraints, overcome phobias, and strive for the remarkable.

I've personally seen the transformational effect of motivational speakers. It's more than just words; it's a strong elixir that revitalizes spirits and guides people through the ups and downs of their personal and professional lives.

In addition to my therapeutic practice, I am a motivational speaker with great passion and purpose. In such a role, I begin each phase of my professional career with a great desire to inspire and uplift my audience.

Why do people seek out motivational speakers like myself? It's not simply the words uttered; it's the bond made, the resonance that comes when shared experiences and insights fit with the listener's own goals. It's a mutually beneficial connection in which I share honest accounts that mirror the problems and victories we all face.

As I begin on this journey as a motivational speaker, I am

motivated by the realization that my words may serve as beacons of hope, illuminating the route for others to traverse their own complexity.

As a result, I approach motivational speaking with a great feeling of duty and purpose. It's a pledge to be a catalyst for good change, a lighthouse that not only lights the way forward but also inspires others to begin on their own paths of self-discovery and accomplishment.

Our journey begins with the realization that emptiness, far from being a dreadful void, is an opportunity—a chance to fill our own spaces with meaning, happiness, and progress. We will unravel the threads of resilience and change woven into the fabric of my experiences via the prism of my own professional journey, which spans numerous fields ranging from teenage mental health to geriatrics and beyond.

Consider this chapter to be a virtual compass pointing in the direction of reflection and empowerment. We'll negotiate the complexities of self-awareness together, finding the shapes of our own Wide Open Spaces ready to be filled. It's a trip that fosters a feeling of community and common knowledge rather than simply individual narratives.

I'm compelled to reveal a component of my professional identity that has given important depth to my journey: my work as a motivational speaker. The goal of donning this mantle is to create a climate in which inspiration becomes the impetus for personal and social development rather than just addressing an audience.

I draw on my experiences in mental health, a sector that has allowed me to interact with people at all phases of their lives. I've realized that emptiness is a multidimensional idea that manifests in the holes left by life's ebbs and flows—whether it's the heartbreaking aftermath of loss, the uncertainties that accompany changes, or the subtle longing for new challenges and undiscovered regions.

Most importantly, I urge reflection on the idea that not all vacant spaces should be viewed negatively. Rather, they should be viewed as potential areas for development, marks of progress, and evidence of an innate desire for something more substantial. These empty areas, like a blank canvas in front of an artist, carry the promise of transformation and the possibility of creating something beautiful and meaningful.

Personal emptiness dynamics are not static; they are dynamic and react to life's rhythms. Accepting our diverse nature helps us to reinterpret our experiences, recognizing that the gaps we meet may be catalysts for positive transformation. They become markers that we have met objectives, attained milestones, or are ready to embark on new undertakings.

It is critical in this investigation to counter the prevalent narrative that links emptiness primarily with negativity. By identifying the good potential inside these holes, we open ourselves up to a world of possibilities and create the path for a development and progress-oriented attitude.

It becomes clear that emptiness is a dynamic force molded by the shapes of our life experiences rather than a static idea. It changes colors and textures in reaction to the tapestry of loss, life changes, boredom, and the natural yearning for new challenges—a mosaic of emotions that echo with the ebb and flow of existence.

I invite you, dear reader, to start on a self-discovery trip by recognizing and pondering on the roots of your own emptiness. These gaps, created by the complicated dance of life's transformations, allow us to look within and unravel the threads that weave the fabric of our emotional landscapes.

In my own path, I've dealt with a recurring issue that has become a defining feature of my life: body image. The origins of this problem may be traced back to my youth when my parents took me to Weight Watchers meetings when I was in fifth grade with good intentions. This well-intentioned action, motivated by our family's history of weight-related health difficulties, unwittingly triggered the formation of a critical inner voice within me.

For over five decades, I listened to this inner voice, especially when comparing my looks to those of my friends. Despite rationally comprehending that their attractiveness was derived from their personality and fitness efforts, the comparison remained a source of emptiness.

During the lockdown, I had a watershed moment in my path. Being able to spend more time at home provided me with the chance to make substantial lifestyle adjustments, notably in my eating habits. Instead of eating out, I had my food delivered from the grocery store, which eliminated unhealthy and bad meal choices.

Surprisingly, this moment of transition provided an unanticipated source of empowerment—I began photographing myself. This act grew into a transforming experience despite my past resistance to being photographed. These photos were not only taken by me but they were also posted on social media sites such as Instagram and Facebook.

While some of my friends misconstrued my activities, believing I was looking for accolades or attention, the truth was considerably more complex. Taking and sharing these photos became a way for me to find and accept myself. It gave me a fresh perspective on myself, allowing me to enjoy the genuine smile that expressed my carefree and cheerful personality.

This personal experience shows the possibility of transformation, even after years of battling with a particular feature of oneself. I was able to replace the void left by my body image issues via lifestyle changes, self-reflection, and a shift in viewpoint.

What I had learned during my transition period was that whether subtle or seismic, life brings with it its own brand of emptiness. When we accept the development of self and situation, we learn that these empty spaces constitute fertile ground for self-discovery and the creation of new narratives. It is an encouragement to change, evolve, and rethink our definition of fulfillment.

The desire for new challenges acts as a light, driving us toward uncharted territory. It is a call to action that speaks to the underlying human desire for progress and achievement. By tackling the emptiness created by a desire for challenges, we place ourselves on the verge of personal and professional growth.

Emptiness, as I've learned from personal and professional

experiences, is not always associated with negativity. Instead, it's a subtle sign that our lives are changing, improving, and always striving for greater heights.

The analogy of an ancient scale comes to mind—the delicate balance we strive for in our lives. Equilibrium, like the scales where one side must not outweigh the other, is essential for a satisfying and peaceful existence. It's a reminder that emptiness, whether it comes from reaching a goal or finishing a chapter in our life, may represent development and the instinctive need to go ahead.

I emphasize the transforming potential of injecting good thoughts and energy into nothingness. It's a conscious decision to see these empty areas as canvases, begging for creative and purposeful strokes. We are actively participating in a process of self-empowerment and progress by doing so.

I invite you to go on a self-discovery trip, finding your own empty spaces. These venues, whether big or small, have the potential for constructive change. It's an invitation to fill these gaps with a combination of imagination and effort. We have the ability to sculpt our experiences, desires, and the very essence of our being, much like an artist does with a blank canvas.

Recognizing the commitment to well-being and happiness has been a transforming journey for me, defined by a profound realization that the work engaged in this process is, at its core, an investment in my own satisfaction.

The recognition that my well-being is inextricably linked to my happiness is the foundation of this commitment. It's about realizing that living a balanced and fulfilling life is a journey in which every step counts. Every choice I make, every moment of self-reflection, and every intentional choice I make to fill the empty spaces inside me contribute to this continual commitment.

This dedication is not without difficulties. On the way to well-being and happiness, there are periods of self-doubt, external pressures, and unanticipated diversions. However, it is during these times that the investment becomes even more important. It is a dedication to resilience, the capacity to recover from failures, and the realization that progress typically results from overcoming obstacles.

As I actively engage in my own pleasure and well-being, I discover that the benefits transcend beyond my own life. It affects how I engage with others, how much energy I bring to relationships, and how much effect I can have on the world around me. It's a ripple effect—an investment that enhances my life.

In my effort to give useful tools for individuals traversing their own wide-open spaces, I'd like to share a useful resource that has greatly aided my personal journey: the Insight Timer app. This software has evolved into a meditation haven, providing a wide range of alternatives such as guided meditations, soundscapes, and more.

One such gem I recently discovered on Insight Timer is a 2011 meditation titled "Where Can I Go?" by Swami NEMADHURAM. This meditation, which is ideally connected with the concept of wide-open spaces, gives a profound experience that I feel will resonate with many people who are looking for introspection and a deeper connection with their inner selves.

As much as I promote this particular meditation, I encourage you to go at your own speed. Allow yourself to be soothed by the relaxing combination of birdsong, music, and flute playing. I discovered that listening to this meditation freed up my creativity and attentiveness. It's a peaceful tour that, in the context of our investigation, perfectly complements the idea of filling our empty places.

Also, let's do a quick yet effective visualization exercise together. I ask you to close your eyes and imagine a peaceful setting while we take a minute to center ourselves. Imagine yourself sitting on the bank of a tranquil lake, the sun gently glinting on the water. Take in the scent of nature as you breathe in. Reach for a nearby fallen leaf and study its vivid green hue, feel its texture, and allow it to recall thoughts or memories.

Extend your focus to the water in front of you. Examine the temperature of the water with your fingertips. Is it warm, chilly, or refreshing? Engage in a thorough investigation of your inner self as you sit in this moment, surrounded by the sounds of the wind in the trees and the soothing waves. Recognize any sensations of emptiness, loss, or untapped potential inside the empty gaps.

As we continue to explore wide-open spaces, both outward and internal, I present an invitation—a call to action that mirrors the core of our introspective trip. I invite each reader to go outdoors and immerse themselves in the tactile beauty of their surroundings, as well as to participate in a meditative discourse with the vast expanses within.

Consider the hues in the sky, the rustling leaves, the patterns on the pavement, or the immensity of your balcony or garden. Allow the breeze to convey the whispers of inspiration. It's in these simple yet meaningful moments that we may begin to discover the holes we want to fill, whether they're vast voids begging for purpose or minor gaps begging for a creative touch.

I recognize that going on this path may seem intimidating, and that's just OK. What matters is that you take that initial step. Begin with a single element, a single location that speaks to you. It may be a creative activity, a period of self-reflection, or a deliberate attempt to bring more good energy into your daily life.

Recognizing the immense potential inside ourselves requires acknowledging that this is not a single task. Seeking professional assistance when necessary is a brave step toward empowerment. As you explore the intricate landscapes of your own wide-open spaces, mental health specialists may give essential insights, direction, and support.

I've stated my profound confidence in the transformational power of positive energy and thoughts throughout this chapter. It's a notion based on the understanding that the energy we put into growing happiness has an impact on our lives. This is more than simply a philosophical position; it is a practical method to influencing our circumstances.

As we explore the undiscovered frontiers of our own potential, let us do so with the firm belief that good change is not only conceivable but also within our reach. Every stride, every effort, and every moment of introspection adds to the collective energy that pulls us forward on our road of self-discovery and satisfaction.

Know that you are not alone in this profound trip as you stand on the threshold of your own wide-open spaces. Embrace the process, take consolation in minor triumphs along the road, and, most importantly, be nice to yourself. We collaboratively navigate toward a future where our wide-open spaces are not foreboding voids to be dreaded by deliberate efforts, a consistent dedication to good energy, and the confidence to seek help when required.

Let us continue to explore, create, and fill the rich landscapes of our lives with the vivid hues of our dreams. The journey continues, and every step, no matter how tiny, adds to the unfolding masterpiece that is our own existence. May the awareness that our potential is limitless motivate us to see wide-open spaces not as obstacles to conquer but as chances for development, satisfaction, and the construction of a life rich in meaning.

Chapter 4 – Notes of Strength Amid Chaos

In crafting each chapter, my intent is clear: to offer a dynamic mix that caters to the diverse needs of my audience. It's not just about disseminating information, nor is it solely a space for mental health discussions. Rather, it's a harmonious blend—a melange of insights, assistance, moments of lightheartedness, and opportunities for relaxation.

My goal in creating each part is to provide a lively blend that meets the wide range of reader demands. This is more than just an intellectual exchange platform; it's a narrative journey that explores the depths of human experience, revealing new levels of comprehension and insight. Let's explore the subtleties that make up this chapter's core as we venture into a world where words serve as a means of communication and discovery.

In the corridors of psychiatric facilities, where the echoes of resilience, struggles, and triumphs reverberate through the air, I have spent years bearing witness to the profound intricacies of the human mind. These experiences have forged an indelible connection to the multifaceted tapestry of mental health—a connection that runs deep and informs the very core of my professional journey.

The complexities I've encountered within those walls have transcended the clinical labels attached to mental health conditions. Instead, they have unfolded as intricate narratives of individuals navigating the labyrinth of their own minds. It's a crucible of emotions and experiences, where the human spirit, in its most vulnerable moments, unveils its resilience in the face of adversity.

In this crucible, I have cultivated a profound understanding—a nuanced comprehension of the delicate dance between mental health and the human experience. It's not just about diagnosing and treating conditions; it's about recognizing the inherent strength within each individual, acknowledging their struggles, and celebrating the triumphs that often emerge as beacons of hope in the darkest of times.

Beyond the sterile gaze of clinical observations, this expedition delves deep into the beating heart of human connection, understanding, and compassion.

The stories etched in the fabric of my experiences form the ink that colors the narrative of this chapter. It's more than a recounting of professional encounters; it's a conscious effort to illuminate a path toward mental well-being and resilience—a path paved with empathy and a deep understanding of the intricacies that define the human struggle.

I set out on a quest to dismantle the obstacles that frequently divide clinical viewpoints from the lived realities of those dealing with mental health difficulties by exposing the subtleties of mental health assistance. It's an appeal to see the human element in all journeys, realizing that every individual traversing the maze of mental health has with them a distinct backstory, a set of difficulties, and a strength that is just waiting to be found.

The conviction that genuine mental health support goes beyond diagnosis and treatment regimens is what drives this purpose. It's about creating a space where people feel heard, seen, and understood. It's about establishing an environment where the complexity of the human experience is addressed with empathy and where pursuing resilience is a shared human goal rather than just a clinical one.

During our research, we came across the fascinating idea of chaos—a complex dance of total disarray and confusion embellished with erratic components yet supported by a recurring pattern.

Chaos, which is frequently connected to disorder and unpredictable behavior, is quite similar to the complex web of human experience. Similar to how life incorporates its erratic aspects into the fabric of who we are, there is an underlying pattern—a delicate harmony—that is apparent when we stand back and look.

I make my way through the maze of chaos by drawing on my experiences, both personal and professional, and realizing that it is a dynamic and unavoidable part of life rather than something to be dreaded. The most transforming events frequently transpire in the midst of turmoil; these are times when we develop and adapt, and unanticipated patterns that become recurring themes in our lives emerge.

I choose to intentionally include my experiences in the larger conversation about chaos rather than sharing this particular chapter only for the sake of catharsis in the embrace of vulnerability. The podcast changed from being a traditional educational session to a poignant and sympathetic investigation of the complex fabric of the human experience.

With all of its subtle emotional undertones, my voyage ended up serving as a prism through which I viewed chaos more broadly. It was about the emotional disruption that comes along with big life events, not simply about chaos and disturbance. Through the integration of my own story with the overarching theme of chaos, the podcast surpassed its intended informative function and evolved into a source of common understanding and community.

I discovered that my emotional journey includes sources that come from reflection and personal hardship. My personal experiences create a vibrant image of coping strategies—a palette full of colors representing self-care, the skill of rephrasing ideas, and the consoling warmth found in the embrace of routines.

The coping strategies I offer on these pages are neither medical recommendations nor cold-call guidance. Rather, they show up as true representations of my own experiences. Each word carries the weight of sincerity, forged in the furnace of enduring the turbulent fallout from loss. It is evidence of the sincere techniques that, in the midst of emotional turmoil, proved to be not only successful but also radically transformational.

The notion of self-care, which is frequently bandied about, has a more complex significance when I consider its part in my own recovery. It's a conscious and caring act of taking care of one's emotional well-being, not just a to-do list. The depth of self-care is examined in this chapter, which also highlights the subtle but significant ways that it became a pillar of my path to resilience.

Through the trial and error of navigating sorrow, the art of reframing ideas arises. It has to do with purposefully turning the mind away from the emotional tempest in order to look for fresh insights. In these pages, I peel back the layers of this cognitive revolution, showing how reframing turned became a compass for locating flashes of insight and optimism.

Routines, which are sometimes undervalued in terms of their importance, take center stage as a comfort. This chapter explores how everyday rhythms provide a familiar embrace and how their consistency acts as an anchor in the face of upheaval. It's evidence of the stabilizing influence routine everyday activities may have on our emotional terrain.

It is important to realize that the chaos I address is not a universal idea as I offer my insights. Just as each of us manages the intricacies of life differently, every one of us has a very distinct capacity for thriving or struggling under chaos. This realization serves as a pillar for our investigation, serving as a warning that every reader will experience the stories in this chapter in a unique way.

Amidst the chaos, an important realization dawns on the value of setting aside time for oneself. This is a basic necessity, especially amid the turbulent currents of hectic life, and not a luxury for people with full schedules. It's an admission that self-care is neglected among everyday responsibilities, which leads to burnout and decreased productivity.

The key is realizing that, even with a hectic schedule, setting aside even 10 minutes a day for activities that encourage mental and physical renewal is an unavoidable investment in our health.

The counsel goes beyond words; it turns into a useful manual for you. Finding what offers serenity and bringing it into everyday life is the main focus, whether that be by engaging in meditation, reading a good book, enjoying music, or engaging in a beloved pastime.

It's a call for self-compassion, acknowledging that our health is an indispensable aspect of our existence. Knowing that chaotic thresholds are unique to each person, I emphasize the value of taking deliberate pauses to maintain equilibrium in the face of life's upheaval.

Significant life events, like the death of my father recently, serve as heartbreaking reminders of how unpredictable life is. My father's loss left significant scars on my entire existence.

The unanticipated event of my father's passing turned into a wildfire that shattered the routines I was accustomed to living by. It was in the midst of this commotion that I had to navigate unfamiliar ground and face unanticipated obstacles that put my resilience to the test.

It was a candid sharing of the challenges faced during these tumultuous times, emphasizing the universal truth that life's disruptions are not selective—they touch each one of us in unique ways.

I aim to encapsulate the essence of these shared experiences, bridging the personal and the universal. It's an acknowledgment that major life events have a profound impact, creating chaos that reverberates across various aspects of our lives. The chaos becomes a tangible force, shaping our perspectives, challenging our resilience, and redefining the narratives we once held.

The chaos that results is linked to the human experience rather than existing in isolation, whether it is due to loss, change, or unanticipated difficulties. Through the shared narratives, I wish to provide you comfort, understanding, and a feeling of community in the midst of life's turbulence.

Navigating the tumultuous waters of chaos requires a set of compass points to guide us through the storm. Let's explore some practical strategies that I've personally found effective in reframing chaos, transforming it from an overwhelming force into a navigable journey.

1. **Reframe Your Thoughts:** In the midst of chaos, the power of reframing thoughts emerges as a formidable ally. It's the art of stepping back, reassessing perspectives, and gaining control over reactive responses. By reframing our thoughts, we open the door to a clearer mindset, enabling us to face challenges with resilience and purpose.

2. **One Task at a Time:** Overwhelming often accompanies chaos, and to counter it, the recommendation is simple yet profound—focus on one task at a time. This approach advocates for staying rooted in the present, completing tasks sequentially, and regaining a sense of control over the immediate surroundings.

3. **Speak to the Positive:** Even within chaos, positive aspects can be found. Shifting the focus towards these elements fosters an optimistic outlook and aids in stress

management. Embracing positivity becomes a powerful tool in the journey through tumultuous times.

4. **Distractions:** Taking a temporary break from overwhelming situations is not a sign of weakness but a strategic move. Distractions, be it a walk, reading a magazine, or engaging in a hobby, provide a mental hiatus, preventing a sense of immobilization and fostering a renewed perspective.

5. **Mindfulness and Breathing:** Amidst the chaos, mindfulness and intentional breathing become anchors. These practices alleviate anxiety, bring calm to the mind, and offer a moment of respite in the storm. The breath becomes a guide, a rhythm that helps navigate through turbulent times.

6. **Socialize:** Despite the chaos, the value of socializing remains paramount. Being in the company of others, sharing experiences, and listening to diverse narratives offer a broader perspective and a sense of connection during difficult moments.

7. **Acknowledge Successes:** Even small victories deserve acknowledgment. Amidst the chaos, recognizing achievements, no matter how modest, contributes to a sense of accomplishment and bolsters self-esteem. It's a reminder that progress, no matter how incremental, is still progress.

8. **Self-Care:** Whether it's enjoying a nutrient-packed smoothie, embracing a new leisure activity, or indulging in a massage, acts of kindness toward oneself are integral to maintaining mental well-being during turbulent periods.

I found solace in the ageless and universally relatable words of songs, even in the middle of upheaval. Allow me to impart to you the knowledge found in "The Climb" by Miley Cyrus and "Carry On" by Fun.

With the stirring words, "There's always going to be another mountain. I'm always gonna want to make it move," Miley Cyrus sets us on a trip. When chaos appears unconquerable, these words have a profound impact. Even if the climb is difficult, it shows how strong and persistent we are. These lines became a moving anthem for me while I went through personal turmoil, serving as a reminder that obstacles are necessary for personal development.

The song "Carry On" by Fun depicts resiliency in striking detail. "If you're lost and alone, or you're sinking like a stone, carry on." Suffering and confusion make it rebellious to continue, to refuse to let the situation define you. The notion of anchoring oneself and letting the past be the echo of our steps on firm ground is captured in this song.

These verses provided comfort during chaotic times, serving as a constant reminder that every obstacle is a chance for personal growth. I urge you to listen to the songs that speak to your experience since we frequently recognize ourselves in the lyrics.

It's critical to acknowledge and rejoice in even the tiny successes. Every victory, no matter how big or small, adds a different note to the life symphony. Whether you've overcome a significant obstacle or just made it through a hectic day, every step you take adds to the complex song of your journey.

A potent affirmation is to ground oneself in the knowledge that you are resilient and courageous by nature. It's an admission that you have the courage to face and conquer obstacles in spite of the mayhem and uncertainty. As you traverse the ups and downs of life, this grounding acts as a stabilizing factor, giving you a sense of rootedness and certainty.

Though the obstacles in life may seem overwhelming, you possess the resilience to overcome them. As you navigate the uncertain road ahead, accept the lessons buried in the chaos, take comfort in the people surrounding you, and keep moving forward with unshakeable faith in your ability to triumph.

This chapter is a celebration of each person's innate resilience rather than merely a discussion on chaos. Thus, celebrate your successes, stay rooted in the here and now, and go on with a determined heart, for the ascent is just as important as the destination, and the trip itself is a victory.

Chapter 5 – How Music Shapes the Journey Within

We discover the deep meaning of music when we lose ourselves in its entrancing world and venture beyond the shallow borders of simple amusement. Beyond the bounds of the aural senses, music is a powerful force that is deeply woven into the fabric of the human experience. Its tentacles stretch deep within us, to the very center of who we are. Music is a transforming medium that elicits emotions, shapes views, and leaves an enduring mark on the canvas of our total well-being in this complex dance between sound and spirit.

Music is now a vital thread that runs across my life. It's a dynamic force that shapes and directs my journey, not just a passive backdrop. Think of it as a quiet walker accompanying me on life's journey, a steady presence.

I learned that music is more than just a fun distraction. It touches the very core of my existence and beyond the auditory. Each composition's rhythms blend with my emotions' cadence to produce a melodic dance that reflects the highs and lows of my inner world.

This musical journey is a profound plunge into the essence of who I am; it's about more than simply sounds and melodies. Every tune turns into a language, conveying emotions and subtleties that words frequently can't explain. The words and harmonies transform into mirrors that reflect the various facets of my soul on this personal trip.

Music acts as a guide in the symphony of life, increasing and molding each moment's emotional impact. It serves as a mirror, reflecting back the intricacies, pleasures, and sufferings that characterize the human condition. I've learned from this continuous investigation that music is a strong force that defines and clarifies the fundamental essence of my being, not merely an outside effect.

While in quarantine, I found myself thinking about how to use my diverse set of abilities and experiences to further a worthwhile project. The concept for a podcast started to take shape, influenced by my experiences in journalism, where narrative is important, and my work as a therapist, where compassionate communication is essential. It developed into a means of bringing these elements together and offering a forum for discussions that speak to the struggles and victories of the human condition.

When my podcast, "Wide Open Spaces with Ilise," first began, a unique intersection of three different professional domains— motivational speaking, therapy, and journalism—led to an unexpected and fortunate development. The tale of the podcast's inception is deeply entwined with the pandemic, which, despite its difficulties, served as a spur for introspective contemplation and aspirations toward transformation.

My storytelling talents as an experienced professional with a background in journalism resonated with the podcasting medium. A platform that broke beyond traditional limits was created by fusing journalistic narratives with the fields of treatment and motivational speaking. It was an organic reaction to the changing dynamics of my environment rather than a planned undertaking.

This blending of abilities and experiences occurred in the crucible of the pandemic, which was characterized by uncertainty and change. The pandemic's insistence on silence and reflection provided a unique opportunity for me to combine my several areas of knowledge into a single, well-rounded project. The outcome was the podcast "Wide Open Spaces," which aims to investigate the unexplored areas in the world and inside each of us.

The unexpected events of the pandemic served as the foundation for my podcast's original story, which blends the therapeutic and empathetic elements of motivational speaking with the storytelling skills, narrative structure, and quest for truth that define journalism. The podcast evolved into a tool for understanding the intricacies of the human experience as well as for sharing experiences.

As a motivational speaker, I understood the ability of words to encourage, uplift, and effect good change. This part of my professional identity evolved naturally into the podcast, where I offered thoughts, anecdotes, and discussions that might inspire inspiration and promote personal development.

During a world crisis, podcasting was a new and exciting endeavor that presented both challenges and rewards. It gave the ambiguities of the times a sense of direction. Every session evolved into an investigation of expansive areas, both outside and internally—areas awaiting the infusion of ideas, coping strategies, and a mutual comprehension of our shared path.

Music is not limited to amusement spaces; instead, it's a lifelong friend who walks behind me while I go about my daily activities. Music is what makes my life what it is, whether I'm eating at a restaurant, browsing the aisles of a store, or just relaxing in a quiet bookshop.

Think about the background music that fills a restaurant, creating an atmosphere and impacting the dining experience. Beyond the culinary delights, the rhythm and music contribute subtly but significantly to the gastronomic experience by boosting tastes and fostering an environment.

In the same way, music stops being just a background hum as I go through malls. It turns into a driving force that directs my movements, establishes a cadence for discovery, and heightens the sensory experience of shopping as a whole. It's more than just a soundtrack; it's a dynamic component that gives the browsing and choosing process life and passion.

Even in the calm areas of a bookshop, music makes its way in, adding a melodic touch to the stillness. A special synergy is created between literary study and melodic sounds, making reading a book a multisensory experience.

I considered study results from the study Marks Institute for Brain and Behavior Development in an effort to comprehend the tremendous effects of music on cognitive processes. The findings of this study provide insight into the complex link between music and cognitive capacities and are quite consistent with my own views and experiences.

Immersing myself in the knowledge gained from this academy confirms what I've felt deep down: music has power that goes beyond simple enjoyment. According to the research, listening to music can activate cognitive processes, improving memory and retention and optimizing learning potential.

Not only is the complex dance between melodies and memory anecdotal but it is also based on scientific investigation. The discovery that listening to music causes certain feelings, memories, and ideas in our brains is intriguing and can have a favorable impact on mental health. This discovery is in perfect harmony with my own conviction that music has the power to change our emotional environment.

Furthermore, the study describes how music fits into the complex symphony of cognitive processes. It's more than simply an audio experience—it's a mental workout that activates different parts of the brain and builds connections that help with memory and recall. The notion that music has the power to optimize our learning capacity gives music a deeper relevance in our lives.

As I take in the results of this research, I feel obligated to apply this information to my own work and personal life. It supports the idea that purposefully integrating music into many facets of life—whether at work or at leisure—can have profound advantages for mental health.

During my research into the interesting relationship between music and the human brain, I read about a popular course offered at the University of Central Florida. This course carefully breaks down how our brains react to different types of music. My personal interest in the complex interplay between music and cognitive function is piqued by the insights gained from this course.

When I picture myself taking this insightful course, I see myself straddling the line between neurobiology and musical expression. I find it intriguing that a neuroscientist and a well-known violinist are collaborating since they provide a multifaceted perspective on how music affects human behavior and brain function.

My eyes widen as I take in all that these instructors have taught me about the impact that music has on our thoughts. The discovery that music may be a powerful stress reliever resonates with me since I have personally turned to music in trying circumstances. Its therapeutic potential gains relevance from the notion that it can reduce pain and feelings of depression.

Additionally, the course explores the cognitive domain and how music improves motor and cognitive abilities. This really speaks to my conviction that music has many positive effects on our bodies and minds, serving not just as a comforting emotional outlet but also as a stimulating force. The idea that music might aid in neurogenesis, spiritual development, and temporal learning piques our curiosity about the profound effects of listening to music on our general well-being.

As I consider these insights, I am motivated to apply this sophisticated comprehension to my own support of music's transformational potential. The University of Central Florida course is a lighthouse, demonstrating the various ways that music may be used to improve our emotional and mental health.

I am enthralled with the raw power contained in the verses of various musicians as I make my way through the world of song lyrics;

each one provides a distinct perspective on how feelings and experiences are expressed.

Consider the beauty of LeAnn Womack's song "I Hope You Dance," which serves as a moving reminder of the human spirit's constant waltz between awe and hunger. The experience of reading the text without the musical accompaniment changes, making the message's main points more profoundly resonant. It is evidence of the inherent power of language, which may arouse a wide range of feelings and encourage reflection.

Tom Petty's resolute proclamation in "I Won't Back Down" resonates with fortitude and unflinching resolve. When the song's melody is removed, the words serve as a rallying call for us to persevere in the face of hardship. This investigation has strengthened my conviction that music lyrics may act as inspirational compass points that help us overcome obstacles in life.

Divorced from its musical counterpart, Taylor Swift's "All Too Well," a poignant song written during a difficult period in her life, becomes a personal declaration of vulnerability. I can relate to the lyrics' unvarnished honesty, which highlights the healing power of songwriting as a form of self-expression. This idea is consistent with my support of the use of creative outlets for mental health.

Without the beachy tunes, Jimmy Buffett's whimsical interpretation of "Margaritaville" takes on a whole new meaning. The song's words become a joyful experience, highlighting the comedy and sense of escape that are inherent in Buffett's narrative. This supports the idea that words have a remarkable capacity to evoke emotions and take us to new mental places even when there is no music present.

And then, when you look at the words of Bon Jovi's hit song "It's My Life," all of a sudden it becomes a personal statement about independence and self-determination. These phrases capture the ability to control our destiny, stand out from the crowd, and live life on our terms. This idea strongly connects with my concept of accepting one's path with agency and purpose.

I am reminded by these lyrical assessments that the beauty of language, free from the constraints of musical notation, has inherent value. It is a weight that cuts beyond genres and historical periods, providing an enduring path for introspection, empowerment, and community.

Together, let's investigate the healing possibilities inherent in the symbiotic relationship between lyrics and feelings—a symbiosis that extends beyond the aural experience and digs deep into each of our unique stories.

Let me assign you a task that is more than simply a chore; it's a road map for reflection and self-awareness. I want you to select music that matches the rhythm of your feelings, music that expresses what's currently going on within your heart. After you've determined which tunes go well together, go one step further and print the lyrics. Yes, the phrases, those lyrical statements that have a strength all their own yet frequently blend inextricably with the tunes.

Take in the complex melodies of the music and let it envelop you, bringing forth the feelings that are captured in its sounds. Then, take the words out of their musical cage and read them with a critical eye at a different time. Take the words and leave them alone, without any melodic background, and see how they speak to you.

It is a thought-provoking exercise, a journey into a world where words take center stage without the use of musical flourishes. By giving you this assignment, I'm not only suggesting something to do; I'm also asking you to have a private conversation with yourself. Through self-discovery, the emotional nuances contained in the lines that could be missed within the symphony of instruments can be unlocked through this approach.

I share this project because it resonates with me personally and because I see the healing power in the combination of lyrics and feelings. For me, this exercise has served as a comfort, a source of inspiration, and a trigger for reflection. My sincere hope is that you will also come to appreciate the distinct resonance that every line has when it is given its own limelight and is separated from the melodies that frequently accompany it.

I urge you, my dear readers, to step up to the challenge—choose songs that speak to the symphony of your feelings, print the lyrics, and discover the profound significance of words cut off from their musical equivalents. This is not only a suggestion; rather, it's an invitation to go on a self-exploration adventure with music serving as your guide.

Let's not undervalue the transforming power contained in the lyrics we frequently sing along to as we weave the complex fabric of our lives. You could unearth underlying layers of motives, feelings, and reflections through this intentional act of involvement.

I support you in this search because I have been through comparable terrain myself. With the strength of reflection and the resonance of well-chosen lyrics, I really hope that you find comfort and a fresh perspective on your own story.

Allow the music to accompany you across these expansive areas, with each note symbolizing the possibility of personal development, healing, and self-discovery. May you discover your special tune in life's symphony, one that connects with your heart's beats and guides you to the deep places inside.

Chapter 6 – Beyond The Crossroads

As we begin a new chapter together, my objective remains constant: to accompany you on your trip, particularly through the undiscovered territory that the pandemic has revealed to us. I share not just my ideas but also the collective tales of my own experiences, those of dear friends, and deep family memories. We build a sense of connectedness in this place, weaving a tapestry of shared encounters and shared resilience.

The crux of this chapter is our common humanity and our connectivity in handling the problems that life throws at us, especially during these challenging times. We uncover the ties that unite us by diving into personal experiences – threads braided with vulnerability, strength, and the common search for well-being.

We navigate the ebbs and flows as a group, not just as spectators but as active participants in a story molded by our collective experiences. It is my honest desire to brighten the way with insights and coping techniques, serving as a beacon of direction in the face of potential uncertainty.

The objective has always been to build a meaningful connection with you, my treasured readers, by digging into my own experiences and those of people in my personal circle of influence. I want to create an intimate environment where empathy develops and a common knowledge of the nuances of our human journey emerges via the prism of personal tales. The strands of connection that link us together in our shared humanity are explained in these narratives.

Perhaps you'll discover reflections of your own experiences, problems, and achievements in the ebb and flow of these shared stories. The core of our humanity may be found in these shared moments, in the realization that we are not alone in the complexities of our particular paths.

You may discover a connection with the lives of my friends and family via the prism of these accounts, identifying components that reflect your own. Empathy develops in this realization, building bridges that transcend individual tales and weave us together in a tapestry of common understanding.

Solutions crafted with care and intention can be found within the shared narratives. These coping strategies are more than just stories; they are real knowledge refined from the crucible of life experiences. The goal is to equip you, dear listeners, with important insights and a toolbox of tactics for dealing with the numerous obstacles that life may throw at you.

Among the techniques, you may come across practical approaches that have withstood the test of time. It might be a daily routine that instills a feeling of regularity, a mindfulness practice that anchors the mind in the midst of upheaval, or the adoption of healthy living choices that have become pillars of strength. These are not one-size-fits-all solutions but rather a wide range of possibilities from which to draw inspiration.

Additionally, mental approaches—mindsets and viewpoints that acted as guiding lights during times of uncertainty—will be investigated. These mental techniques, whether establishing a positive perspective, embracing adaptation, or creating a grateful mentality, are powerful tools for navigating the complicated dance between hardship and resilience.

The goal is not to impose a fixed formula but rather to show a mosaic of options. Consider these coping methods to be parts of a puzzle, ready to be rearranged and fitted to the specific contours of your own path.

Work-Life Balance Changes:

The usual boundaries between work and home life were significantly altered during the pandemic. For many, remote work has become the norm, blurring the barriers between professional and personal environments. Recognizing this transition, people began to investigate and apply changes to achieve a healthy work-life balance. Establishing discrete workspaces within houses, outlining clear working hours, and creating habits that allow for mental disengagement from work-related pressures during non-working hours might all contribute to this.

Hobby and Interest Development:

The conscious pursuit of hobbies and interests has arisen as a coping method that goes beyond mere diversion. Participating in activities that offer joy, contentment, and a sense of success has become an essential component of self-care. These deliberate endeavors, whether rediscovering a long-lost love or delving into wholly new territory, serve as antidotes to the monotony and stress of daily living. Individuals found comfort and refreshment in the growth of hobbies, which ranged from creative undertakings to physical activities.

Leisure and Recreation:

Lifestyle changes included a more aware attitude to leisure and recreation. People investigated local jewels, picturesque locations, and recreational routes in their immediate environs due to limits on travel and social activities. This not only improved physical health but also promoted a greater respect for the surrounding environment. It underlined the value of appreciating modest pleasures and finding delight in the familiar.

Holistic Health Practices:

Lifestyle changes went beyond specific activities to holistic health practices. Adopting healthy eating habits, including regular physical activity into daily routines, prioritizing enough sleep, and exploring mindfulness techniques such as meditation or yoga might all contribute to this. These changes help to overall well-being by addressing not just current issues but also building long-term resilience.

Boundaries and Digital Detox:

In an era dominated by digital connections, people understood the necessity for purposeful detachment. Setting screen time limits, adopting digital detox times, and encouraging face-to-face contact (even if virtual) become critical components of lifestyle changes. This deliberate approach to technology usage was designed to reduce the possible negative effects on mental health and foster a healthy relationship with digital platforms.

Lifestyle changes made during the pandemic were proactive

answers to the changing terrain of our lives rather than reactive ones. These deliberate adjustments, suited to individual needs and circumstances, indicate a dynamic response to challenges and a dedication to overall well-being.

Purpose of the Podcast:

It's critical to underline that I don't mean to provide a one-size-fits-all answer in our discussion on coping methods. Instead, consider these coping mechanisms to be a bright mosaic, with each piece representing a possible aspect of resilience and well-being.

A Mosaic of Options:

Consider these coping tactics as a mosaic of options rather than hard prescriptions. Each strategy, whether it's developing hobbies, changing work-life balance, or emphasizing mental health practices, contributes to the coping puzzle. The beauty of these techniques is their adaptability and flexibility, which allows you to choose and mix them based on your specific circumstances.

Pieces of a Puzzle:

Consider each coping technique to be a puzzle piece ready to be strategically positioned inside the bigger picture of your life. Coping, like a puzzle, takes careful assembly to reveal the entire image; similarly, coping necessitates a process of discovery and personalization. Your trip is unique, and the efficiency of these components is determined by how well they correspond to your choices, values, and circumstances.

Personalized Rearrangement:

Your coping journey is a living puzzle, and you have the authority to rearrange the parts as your requirements change. What works now may change over time, which is entirely natural. The goal is not to follow a set formula but to enable you to create a coping method that is unique to you. So, my dear friend, feel free to play around with, change, and customize these parts to make a mosaic that reflects your particular story.

Tailored to Your Journey:

Recognize that your path is unique, and the coping techniques offered are adaptable tools designed to be customized to your circumstances. There is no need to fit into a pre-defined mold; instead, embrace the flexibility to play with these components and find the arrangement that provides you with the most comfort, resilience, and fulfillment.

An Ongoing Investigation:

Coping is a never-ending adventure, and the riddle of well-being is an ongoing investigation. Consider these mechanisms to be invitations to self-discovery and progress. Be patient with yourself, understanding that finding the correct arrangement may take some time. The aim is development and a sense of empowerment in handling life's problems, not perfection.

Inspiration from Robert Frost's Poem:

On this voyage of self-reflection and personal improvement, I am inspired by Robert Frost's immortal poem "The Road Not Taken."

The idea of being at a crossroads with two options connects strongly with the decisions we confront in our own lives. Join me as we investigate the relevance of these two paths and the influence they have on our own narratives.

Standing at the Crossroads:

Imagine yourself standing at a symbolic crossroads in your life, much as Frost's narrator views two different pathways in a golden grove. This junction depicts a point of choosing, where options emerge and various routes beckon. It represents your ability to direct the direction of your adventure.

Visualizing Your Divergent Paths:

Close your eyes and see the two routes ahead of you. The comfort of the known is represented by one, well-trodden and familiar. The unknown, with its difficulties and opportunities, beckons on the less frequented path. I just have to say that, my friend, as you stand at this crossroads, consider the intricacies of each path, as well as the sentiments and expectations they elicit.

Personal Crossroads:

Let's now apply this vision to your own life. Remember times when you had to make critical decisions, similar to the two roads in the poem. Consider the decisions that brought you to where you are now, as well as the lessons learned at those crossroads. You acquire insights into your decision-making tendencies and the influence of those choices on your path by reflecting on your own crossroads.

The Well-Traveled Road:

One road may symbolize the known, the tried and true, and the comfort zone. Consider times when you picked the less traveled path. What were the reasons for their decisions? How did they help your development or, conversely, inhibit your exploration? Recognize the importance of these options in delivering stability and security.

The Path Less Traveled:

On the other hand, consider the times when you took the path less traveled. These are the times of danger, novelty, and venturing beyond one's comfort zone. What did you learn on this less-traveled path? How did it shape your resilience and adaptability? Recognize the bravery required to venture into an unfamiliar area.

Decision-Making Agency:

The ability to choose is a vital part of the human experience. Accept the power you have in navigating your own crossroads. Every decision, whether it leads down a known or unknown road, adds to the changing fabric of your life. Your decisions are more than mere emotions; they are deliberate stages in constructing your unique story.

Learning from Crossroads:

Crossroads are more than simply decision points; they are also chances for learning and growth. Consider the lessons contained in the trip as you picture these various pathways. What personal strengths did you discover? How did difficulties become stepping stones? The paths you've taken have shaped you into the robust, adaptive person you are today.

Moving Forward with Intention:

With this crossroads investigation, I encourage you to approach future decisions with intention. Recognize the opportunity for progress on both well-traveled and less-traveled roads. Whether you select familiarity or novelty, make your decision with your beliefs, objectives, and the narrative you want to create in mind.

Taking the Road Less Traveled

Beginning the path of challenging oneself and stepping beyond one's comfort zone is a transforming quest analogous to opening the gates to personal progress. This fundamental notion is based on the realization that progress, self-discovery, and increased fulfillment frequently lay beyond the boundaries of familiarity.

The Comfort Zone as a Starting Point:

When considering the concept of pushing oneself, it is critical to recognize the comfort zone as a familiar starting place. It's the zone where routines provide security and judgments accord with the known. Consider times in your life when your comfort zone functioned as a foundation, offering stability and ease.

Recognizing the Need for Progress:

At the heart of the human experience lies a natural need for self-discovery and progress. Consider occasions when you sensed a gentle invitation to venture beyond the bounds of familiarity as I present this viewpoint. This might be a slight pull or a strong urge to venture into unfamiliar territory, both emotionally and professionally.

The Catalyst for Change:

Challenges are the catalysts that move us ahead on our journey of personal and professional development. They can take the shape of a new project at work, a shift in duties, or even personal goals that need to be realized. Although overwhelming, but dear friends, these obstacles have the potential to become stepping stones toward a more meaningful and satisfying existence.

Overcoming Fear of the Unknown:

The lack of dread connected with the unknown is one of the intrinsic properties of the comfort zone. Taking the next step means addressing uncertainty and accepting the potential of failure. Consider times when your fear of the unknown was a hindrance. How did you overcome your anxieties, and what did you learn as a result of your experiences?

Uncharted Territory:

Uncharted territory represents the areas beyond the familiar, where development and transformation await. In your reflections, tell me about times when you purposefully opted to explore the unknown. What did you learn about yourself, your strengths, and your resilience? Consider the value of exploring these unexplored places.

Learning From Hurdles:

Obstacles are not only hurdles; they are also excellent instructors. Every struggle is a chance to learn about oneself, one's abilities, and the tactics that promote resilience. As we go through this process, remember specific obstacles that provided vital insights and opened the path for personal and professional progress.

The Evolutionary Power of Choices:

Decisions made outside of our comfort zone have the unique ability to create our own story. Share your experiences in making brave and unorthodox decisions. What role did these decisions have in your evolution? My friend, it is crucial to recognize your agency in past decisions and the impact they had in shaping who you are now.

Fostering a Mindset of Potential:

Beyond facing problems and making decisions, fostering a mentality of potential is essential for welcoming the unknown with open arms. Consider times when a shift of viewpoint turned adversity into an opportunity. How can we foster a mentality that sees problems as opportunities for growth rather than impassable barriers?

Setting Intentional Challenges:

When challenged consciously, it becomes a tool for shaping the future. Share your opinions on how to establish purposeful challenges that match your aims and contribute to your overall goals. What distinguishes these obstacles from the unexpected, and what role do they play in determining your path?

Meditate on your reflections throughout this investigation of challenging yourself and making decisions outside of your comfort zone. Your experiences, thoughts, and opinions add to the collective wisdom that we are constructing together.

Allow me to create a representation of the fundamental notion of challenging oneself on the canvas of my own experiences—the worlds of job decisions, relationship choices, and personal progress. Each narrative demonstrates the transforming effect of stepping beyond one's comfort zone.

Career Choices:

In the midst of my professional journey, I came to a fork in the road that required me to make a decision outside of my comfort zone. The temptation of stability called from a well-trodden road, but the need for advancement compelled me to venture into unfamiliar territory. When I decided to change careers, I welcomed the discomfort of the unknown. Though intimidating at first, this decision proved a stimulus for skill diversification, increasing my knowledge, and eventually building a more robust professional identity.

Relationship Choices:

Navigating the treacherous terrain of relationships brought its own set of forks in the road. The comfort zone screamed familiarity, but the promise of meaningful relationships encouraged a foray into uncharted emotional terrain. I found the richness that openness and shared experiences offer to relationships by forcing myself to build deeper connections. Each decision to venture beyond my relational comfort zone became a chapter in my own progress story.

Personal Development:

Personal growth voyage occurred via conscious choices to disrupt the existing quo. Every step outside the familiar, from developing new interests to accepting opportunities that challenged my talents, contributed to the shaping of my character. The agony of confronting personal limitations became the fuel that propelled me toward a more real and fulfilled version of myself.

Lessons Discovered:

These personal examples act as stepping stones in a bigger story, providing lessons gained via the prism of real-life situations. Career choices emphasize the value of professional adaptation. Relationship choices disclose the depth created in vulnerability, and personal progress emphasizes the dynamic nature of self-discovery. Through these experiences, I've realized that pushing oneself is a lived reality that determines the outlines of a meaningful and worthwhile existence.

The Ripple Effect:

As I think on my journey of pushing myself, I notice the ripple impact it has. Decisions taken in the heat of suffering not only form my own story but also have an impact on the lives of people around me. It inspires a communal attitude of development, resilience, and the quest for authenticity by inviting people to reflect on their own decisions.

Your Own Personal Adventure:

Imagine the distinct landscapes you want to visit as you begin on your personal voyage into the regions of challenging yourself. Whether it's a professional decision, a relationship decision, or a personal growth quest, each decision becomes a brushstroke on the canvas of your life. Accept the uncertainty, enjoy the discomfort, and love the richness that emerges when you move beyond the familiar.

Visualization Exercise

Consider yourself at a crossroads, a fork in the road with two unique ways ahead of you. This visualization is more than simply a game; it is an investigation of your own willingness to face obstacles and choose the road less traveled.

As I stand at this crossroads, I see a duality of alternatives, each with its own attraction and uncertainty. A well-worn route extends out to the right, familiar, comfortable, and paved by the footsteps of those who have walked it before. The sun shines through the forest canopy, providing a pleasant warmth on the well-worn path. It symbolizes the safe, recognized path of least resistance.

A less-traveled road runs through the wild forest to the left. The grass is rich underfoot, and the surroundings are more wild and unpredictable. The shadows dance on the uneven ground, representing the uncertainty and probable difficulties that lie ahead. This road represents uncharted territory, personal progress, and the appeal of embracing the unknown.

The feelings that arise within you as you stand at this crossroads with me. Are you lured to the well-worn route because it represents comfort and familiarity? Or does the appeal of the less-traveled path grab your soul and pique your interest in the unknown? Recognize and accept your current intuition and sentiments.

The significance of this picture is not only the choice you make but also the recognition of your own readiness. Are you ready to face the obstacles of taking the road less traveled? Is the call to expand and explore louder than the comfort of the known? This is a profoundly personal journey, and your selection should reflect your unique goals and level of preparation.

Allow the imagery to crystallize in your mind as you imagine these diverse routes. Feel the texture of the ground beneath your feet, the warmth of the sun, and the rustle of leaves in the air. This activity invites you to reflect, analyze your own tendencies, and enjoy the dynamic interaction between preparedness and challenge.

Recognize, at this moment of thought, that preparedness is not a static condition; it changes with time and experience. What appears to be a difficult route now may become a well-trodden one tomorrow. The familiar, on the other hand, may evolve into the unknown. This ambiguity is inherent in the human experience, and your journey is entirely unique to you.

So, take a deep breath and let yourself get immersed in this vision. Stand at the crossroads with purpose, aware of the gravity of your decisions. Embrace the duality of the routes before you, and let the images direct you to a better awareness of your own preparedness to take on new challenges and evolve.

Decision-Making and Coping Skills

When confronted with the perplexing dance of decision-making, I take refuge in the ordered simplicity of creating pros and cons lists. This age-old strategy, which is sometimes regarded as too simple, acts as my compass in navigating the maze of options. Let me share with you the process of weighing possibilities, which has been a constant companion throughout my trip.

As I stand at the crossroads of options, the pros and cons lists unroll in front of me like parchment, displaying the possible results of each path. On one side, the pros, embellished with promises of happiness and money, build a picture of the advantages that await. Simultaneously, the cons, harsh and unrelenting, exposed the possible difficulties, prompting me to proceed carefully.

The act of outlining these lists is a type of thoughtful artwork as much as a practical activity. Each entry adds to the unfolding masterpiece of choice. The beauty of the method rests in its simplicity—it's a discussion with oneself, an opportunity to reflect and explore the complexities of what lies ahead.

Precision is essential in the compilation of these lists. I consider not just observable variables but also subtle whispers of intuition and emotion. It's a delicate interplay of logic and emotion, a hint of discernment between the heart and head. This approach necessitates honesty—confronting prejudices, admitting worries, and celebrating goals.

Patterns arise when I examine the pros and cons lists, showing the dimensions of my aspirations and apprehensions. This visual portrayal of possibilities provides me with clarity—like a lantern in the dark hallways of doubt. Each pro and con is a voice in the decision-making chorus, harmonizing to lead me to sound decisions.

However, it is critical to understand that these lists are not unchangeable rules but rather adaptable recommendations. They give a picture of my ideas at a certain point in time, reflecting my comprehension at the time. The fluidity of decision-making, like the ever-changing waves, necessitates the willingness to revisit these lists as circumstances change.

Throughout the course of my journey, I've discovered that decisions are not discrete occurrences but rather threads sewn throughout the fabric of life. The lists of pros and drawbacks are tools, not tyrants, and are intended to empower rather than limit. It's a dance of discernment, a conversation with oneself that grows with each decision.

The route of self-discovery and intentional decision-making corresponds to the core of personal development—a journey I enthusiastically support. I've observed that the decisions that resonate with the resonance of growth are frequently the ones that result in the most significant transformations. Allow me to share with you the enormous influence that making decisions in accordance with personal growth has had on my path.

I encourage you to push yourself and see each decision as a stepping stone in the mosaic of your own development. The act of pushing oneself is an expression of resilience and a demonstration of faith in one's own ability for improvement. It takes deliberate action to break out from the familiar's inertia and embrace the rich ground of the unfamiliar.

When I think back on my own critical moments, I notice a constant thread: the desire to venture into the unknown, face the discomfort of uncertainty, and the ambiguity that comes with progress. Whether it was a professional change, a relationship decision, or the pursuit of a passion, each decision to question the status quo served as a spark for broader growth.

Aligning decisions with personal growth necessitates a certain amount of audacity—the willingness to shed the old skin of familiarity and embrace the raw vibrancy of new possibilities. It's not about making choices for the sake of change but about making decisions that reflect the person you want to be.

Throughout this journey, I've discovered that growth frequently occurs in the spaces between comfort and suffering. Dormant potentials awaken at times of difficulty, and dormant seeds of change blossom. Choosing growth is a self-nurturing act, a decision to tend your potential garden and enable it to thrive and bloom.

You need to regard the decisions before you as sacred possibilities for growth rather than just pragmatic choices. Push the bounds of what you know, journey into the unknown, and allow your decisions to serve as a compass pointing you toward the broad horizons of your own progress.

When I think back on my own experiences, I recall times of meaningful decision-making, such as adapting professional approaches to the virtual terrain, reevaluating personal priorities, and nurturing relationships in novel ways. The pandemic forced me to confront decisions that I would have avoided under normal circumstances. It was a moment of transformation, and each decision served as a stepping stone in the growth of resilience and flexibility.

Think through your personal experiences throughout this epochal period, as well as the decisions that established your path. How did you deal with the uncertainty? What decisions did you make that aided your personal development? The pandemic's obstacles were, in essence, a crucible for growth, testing our fortitude and challenging us to choose pathways that matched our innermost ideals.

This thought is not about lingering on the difficulties encountered but rather about acknowledging the fortitude discovered in the furnace of difficulties. It's an opportunity to reflect on the choices that, in retrospect, were crucial in forming the person you've become. Each choice taken during this unusual moment adds richness and texture to the expanding tapestry of personal and collective experiences, whether it was adopting new methods of working, cultivating resilience in the face of hardship, or recalibrating personal objectives. These actions, whether monumental or apparently little, collectively define the narrative of resilience, adaptability, and development emerging from the ordeal.

In these trying times, I advocate for deliberate decision-making, recognizing the power we have to shape the course of our lives. It's not just about the destination but about embracing the entire trip and appreciating every step done, regardless of the road selected.

In an unpredictable environment, when extraordinary occurrences transform the globe, the capacity to make conscious decisions becomes a compass guiding us through new territory. It's about realizing that, in the face of external problems, our internal decisions have the power to shape our narratives.

It is a genuine acknowledgment of the vast richness buried in the multiplicity of experiences. Every choice I make adds to the complex tapestry of my personal development and resilience.

I see my decisions as my own progress as I navigate the intricacies of life during these unusual times. My pandemic story is studded with moments of courage, perseverance, and the ongoing process of self-discovery.

I want to leave you with a deep realization: the decisions I make today are more than just markers in the present; they are the builders of my future. Every decision, every step down this winding road, contributes to the pattern for what is to come.

This is a call to action, not just an intellectual notion. I am prompted to engage in deliberate self-reflection, to examine my decisions not with a critical eye but with a desire to comprehend their ramifications. The difficulties that I face are not hurdles; they are chances for personal progress, periods in which I may construct and enhance the story of my life.

It's a story of perseverance, flexibility, and the unflinching determination to see setbacks as opportunities for progress. This chapter serves as a reminder that each struggle represents an opportunity to add richness and brightness to my life. With this perspective, I take a step ahead, not as a passive viewer of life, but as an active player.

Chapter 7 – In the Mirror of Self-Reflection

My dear readers, imagine the Looking Glass as a tool designed to help you traverse the complex maze of your thoughts and emotions, not merely as a reflected surface. My podcast evolved as a combination of my therapeutic insights and journalistic skills as I ventured into unknown territory. It provides a special mix of observations, wisdom, and coping strategies that are customized for our new world.

It honors resiliency and acknowledges the power that comes from facing challenges as a group. This chapter transforms the Looking Glass from a mirror into a compass that guides us toward development, comprehension, and healing.

Explore a world where the Looking Glass turns into a transformational instrument that provides deep insights in addition to reflections. As a reaction to the changing dynamics of our reality, it is a specially designed navigation system for our modern problems. Discover a carefully selected blend of insights, condensed knowledge, and workable coping mechanisms here, all specifically designed to address the subtleties of our modern society.

Anxiety in the Spotlight

Throughout the previous year, "anxiety" has become ingrained in our common consciousness, weaving itself into the fabric of our shared experience. What was once a phrase reserved for talks about clinical issues has evolved into a general word that permeates all aspects of our lives. Anxiety is no longer confined to the dark corners; it has become a powerful force that can be sensed in everyday interactions, online debates, and even the oblique undertones of social media ads.

This transformation reflects a fundamental shift in how we view and interact with our emotional environments, not just a language evolution. Over time, anxiety has evolved beyond its clinical associations to become a common, age-, gender-, and background-neutral sensation. It's no longer a taboo subject; instead, it's become a major theme in our shared story, influencing our attitudes, discussions, and even how we use technology.

A Personal Exploration of Anxiety's Evolution

Anxiety permeates all aspects of our lives, as demonstrated by the subtle nuances of our interactions as well as the overt debates we have. It shows up as the undefinable hesitancies of an online encounter, the silent anxieties that reverberate in the back of our thoughts when we browse social media, and the tacit understanding that people from different backgrounds have for one another. Recognizing the existence of anxiety is the first step in creating a more understanding and helpful community that successfully navigates the challenges of contemporary life, as it becomes an essential component of our shared experience.

Following the revolutionary events that have transpired since April 2020, I have closely studied and thought about the elevated conversations and raised consciousness of anxiety. An unanticipated trigger, the pandemic, brought anxiety to the fore of our collective awareness and made us reevaluate its cultural assumptions and historical foundations.

Around the world, people were facing previously unheard-of difficulties at this time, which led to an increase in discussions about mental health. Due to the pandemic's widespread effects on our everyday lives, there was a collective realization of the emotional toll it took, which resulted in a wider acceptance of anxiety as a common and legitimate issue.

I must acknowledge the variety of ways that anxiety manifests itself, as well as the shifting tides of society's perceptions about this complicated emotion as I chart its historical development. The way that people see and talk about anxiety has changed from being whispered in the background to being in the open.

The stigma that formerly surrounded anxiety and painted it as a closely kept secret linked to weakness is starting to fade. Throughout these conversations, I have seen preconceived ideas that portrayed anxiety as a weakness in the armor of experts, parents, or strong people gradually crumble. The acceptance of anxiety as a common human feeling, as opposed to a sign of weakness, has grown to be essential to our shared story.

When we consider the social perspective of anxiety and its historical development, we embark on a centuries-long journey. Anxiety has taken on a variety of guises throughout history, from misdiagnosed illness to disregarded annoyance. Over the course of history, public perceptions of anxiety have changed, reflecting the altering tides of cultural, medical, and psychological knowledge.

Earlier periods sometimes shrouded anxiety in mysticism, believing it to be the result of supernatural powers or heavenly disapproval. As medical knowledge grew over time, anxiety became more deeply woven into the larger picture of mental health, moving from a mystique to a more complex understanding based on psychology and physiology.

However, despite these developments, society's concept of anxiety remained nuanced. A common theme across historical narratives was the framing of anxiety as a sign of weakness on the part of the individual. The deep-rooted stigma associated with mental health difficulties, such as anxiety, has caused many to struggle with these problems in solitude, away from the critical eyes of society.

It took a massive cultural change to break the stigma associated with anxiety, one that destroyed the long-held belief that anxiety equates to weakness and challenged preconceived beliefs. The difficult path toward de-stigmatization has been paved with the brave voices of those who dared to speak candidly about their experiences. It's crucial to understand that removing these obstacles is a continuous effort that entails promoting empathy, understanding, and a shared commitment to debunking falsehoods that uphold the stigma as we negotiate this historical narrative.

The Waves of Change

These chapters disrupt the formerly dense and oppressive silence around anxiety. This story breaks down barriers, gives voice to those who may not otherwise be heard, and highlights how similar our problems are. It explores the ubiquity of anxiety and reveals the subtle ways in which it affects our emotional and mental environments.

This chapter also explores the ways in which society has changed the way that it views anxiety. Anxiety is no longer relegated to quiet conversations or written off as a specialized issue; instead, it is now a major part of our consciousness. It's a change that calls for both personal reflection and a larger cultural reevaluation of how we view, interact with, and assist individuals who are experiencing anxiety.

It is hard to separate the significant influence of the global disruptor—pandemic—from the beginning of our podcast's journey, as I consider. This seismic event not only altered the course of our everyday lives, but it also, strangely, gave us the freedom to talk honestly about and identify our anxiety. Come along with me as we explore the psychological terrain that the pandemic has shaped and chart the development of our shared experience.

Early in the pandemic, "Wide Open Spaces with Ilise" became a companion for people navigating the unknown waters of uncertainty as the world struggled with the abrupt shift. We started a trip together through this podcast, one that took place in the context of imprisonment, the ebb and flow of diversions, and the gradual but widespread formation of a collective anxiety psychosis.

Lockdowns turned the confinement into a furnace, bringing our internal battles to light. We saw how the human mind navigated the tides of change, from the monotony of isolation to the din of contradicting information. During this time, anxiety stopped being a quiet phantom and instead became a tangible presence that demanded recognition and comprehension.

As a Podcaster and Recreational Therapist, my function grew beyond that of an observer; I started acting as a platform for voices to reflect on the many ways that people have dealt with uncertainty. The episodes woven together tales of vulnerability, resiliency, and the many ways people dealt with their fears, creating a tapestry of our common humanity.

Demystifying Anxiety

The unwritten agreement portrayed anxiety as a weakness, a flaw in the armor, especially reserved for parents, professionals, or those who are seen to be uncompromising. However, the pandemic acted as a disruptor, gradually tearing down the long-standing stigma associated with anxiety. Come along with me as we explore how perspectives are changing and how anxiety is becoming more accepted. This process has been facilitated by the experiences of others who, when faced with extraordinary obstacles, found strength in being vulnerable.

In the not-too-distant past, whispered secrets and hushed talks were the only places where anxiety was allowed to express itself. I want you to think about how the pandemic changed things and how anxiety became more and more of a common experience as we go through this chapter together. I also started to peel back layers of stereotypes and saw that being vulnerable is a sign of our common humanity rather than a sign of weakness.

A new reality where acknowledging anxiety was an expression of strength rather than a sign of fragility was imposed onto professionals, parents, and people from all walks of life. Through our discussions on

"Wide Open Spaces with Ilise," I developed into a voice for stories that went against the conventional wisdom about mental health. The podcast episodes served as a forum for people who, maybe for the first time, felt comfortable talking about their anxiety and realized that vulnerability is what makes us strong.

We set out on a journey that reflects the way anxiety has evolved in society from a stigmatized personal weakness to an acknowledged common feeling. Many were forced into a condition of isolation during the early stages of the pandemic when the accustomed diversions that kept us from facing our deepest fears were removed. During this time, even the most dynamic people, who were used to moving constantly, found themselves in reflective silence, confronting the subtleties of their own nervous thoughts.

I saw this recognition come to all of us. The stories told on the program reflected the feelings of a society experiencing a significant shift in how it views anxiety. I was captivated by the accounts of those who, in the stillness of their alone, faced their fears head-on and peeled back the layers of intricacy that had long been hidden by the everyday grind.

Each episode of my podcast acted as a stepping stone as I traced my own journey through the maze of anxiety, exposing not only the complexities of my own experiences but also giving brave guests a stage on which to tell their gripping tales. In my role as host, I had to walk a tightrope between journalistic curiosity and sympathetic comprehension, fostering an environment where openness turned into strength.

The show's guests shared stories that revealed the unvarnished truths of anxiety and covered the gamut of human emotions. Every narrative, from professionals battling the demands of their positions to parents juggling the difficulties of raising a family in the face of uncertainty, became a mosaic piece adding to the greater image of our common human experience.

The investigation of anxiety transformed into a group effort, dismantling the barriers that had separated it as a personal battle. We discovered the connections between us all via these exchanged tales, understanding that anxiety is a universal component of the human experience rather than a specific flaw. It was a path of self-discovery, comprehension, and, in the end, freedom from the bonds of shame.

The Pandemic as a Precipitating Factor

Anxiety was felt on a tangible level as the pandemic spread around the world. Through my therapeutic observations, I have personally seen the devastating effects of this worldwide upheaval on people's mental environments. The early going was characterized by anxiety, uncertainty, and a feeling of unfamiliar terrain. The daily routines that were used to them were upset, and the coping strategies that had previously worked well were put to the test.

By taking the first-person viewpoint, I become more than just the storyteller; I become a fellow passenger on this turbulent adventure. The pandemic turned into a furnace that tried the mental fortitude of our society as a whole, and the rise in worry was unmistakably a reflection of this furnace. It created a strong urge for introspection and a mental expedition to face long-standing fears that were hiding in the shadows.

After the psychological fallout from the pandemic, there has been a noticeable change in the way society regards mental health. The formerly silent discussions about anxiety, sadness, and other mental health concerns have become more than whispers and oblique references. These days, mental health is a topic of open discussion and a crucial component of the larger social conversation.

This is not only a philosophical shift; it takes the form of concrete manifestations, such as cutting-edge tools, treatments, and merchandise made to tackle the complex aspects of anxiety. Driven by the pandemic, the digital tsunami has flooded us with a plethora of mental health applications, virtual education programs, and devices designed to ease anxiety. The availability of mental health services has increased to previously unheard-of heights in our technological age.

Following the digital revolution, accessibility emerged as a key component of mental health services. Therapy apps have become virtual havens, providing people with a private, quick way to consult professionals. It was revolutionary to be able to communicate with certified therapists from the comfort of one's own home since it removed obstacles that could have discouraged people from seeking treatment in the past.

Concurrently, the popularity of online courses skyrocketed, offering organized and instructive methods for understanding and treating anxiety. These classes offered a variety of tools and techniques that people might use in their everyday lives, catering to different learning styles. Whether it was through stress management strategies, mindfulness exercises, or cognitive-behavioral techniques, these courses equipped students with the knowledge to manage their mental health.

Another aspect of this paradigm-shifting wave is the creative explosion of devices designed to reduce anxiety. These gadgets, which range from transcendental meditation to snap bands, relaxing strips, to audio novels, show how technology and mental health can coexist. Coping mechanisms, previously a mysterious field, are now more widely available, providing people with a wide range of tools to help them deal with the challenges associated with maintaining their mental health.

The media have significantly shaped the narrative around mental health in all of its manifestations. TV programs, news articles, and social media initiatives have aided the destigmatization of mental health concerns. A feeling of community and understanding has been cultivated by the amplification of many perspectives, including those of people who have successfully navigated their own mental health journeys.

Tools and Resources for Coping

Apps for meditation have become a potent weapon in the fight for mental health. The ease with which one can now obtain mindfulness exercises, relaxation methods, and guided meditation sessions via a smartphone has revolutionized the way people interact with their mental health. Many now consider meditation a useful and essential part of their everyday lives because of the applications' mobility and user-friendly interfaces that have democratized access to activities that were once seen to be arcane.

The podcast episodes explore and analyze several therapy principles that provide special methods for comprehending and treating anxiety. These ideas offer frameworks for people to investigate the causes of their fears and create coping mechanisms, whether they are applied in dialectical behavior therapy, cognitive-behavioral therapy, or other cutting-edge modalities. The field of therapy is changing, incorporating a range of methods that speak to people's particular needs and preferences.

Another aspect of the digital wave is online courses, which offer an organized route for introspection and development. These classes equip students with useful tools and abilities in addition to teaching them about worry and its subtleties. Accessible expert-led courses have made mental health education more widely available and have promoted a culture of lifelong learning and personal development.

It is impossible to overestimate the influence of technology on the availability of mental health resources. In addition to making therapeutic materials more widely available, the digital wave has eliminated obstacles to getting treatment. A paradigm change in the way we approach mental health assistance has resulted from people being empowered to take proactive measures toward their mental well-being through the anonymity and convenience provided by technology.

When we consider the advantages and future possibilities of these tools, it is clear that the field of mental health is going through a revolutionary change. In addition to providing comfort during difficult times, these resources provide chances for individual development and self-discovery. The development and promotion of these tools by all parties demonstrates a shared commitment to promoting a society in which mental health is valued and available to all.

Self-Awareness Mirror Exercise

This exercise goes beyond the traditional idea of using a mirror to examine one's physical appearance; instead, it explores the metaphysical and invites you to consider the core of your being.

Identifying and modifying one's aura is a fundamental aspect of this practice. The word "aura" is frequently used to describe an ethereal energy or atmosphere that envelops a person. It stands for the combination of ideas, feelings, and self-perceptions that form your inner world in the setting of the self-awareness exercise. Gaining awareness of your aura allows you to see the finer points of your inner environment.

Let's now explore the mirror exercise's practical procedures. Locate a peaceful, cozy area where you may practice contemplation without interruptions. Step in front of a mirror, face yourself and set aside preconceived ideas. Look at your mirror and note any ideas or feelings that come up. It's a chance to face the silent parts of yourself, a moment of unadulterated honesty.

Pay attention to the minute variations in your facial expressions, the feelings that flit across your glance, and the narratives your eyes convey. Give yourself permission to just be there, judgment-free, with whatever comes up. Acceptance and self-compassion are welcome here.

Regular exercise in the mirror practice may have a profoundly transformational effect on your self-awareness. It becomes a ritual of self-love and self-discovery to face oneself in the mirror. You can achieve personal growth and a closer bond with your true self by recognizing and comprehending the reflections inside.

Taking Control of Your Mental Health

In order to emphasize how important personal empowerment is, it is necessary to address the field of mental health. This journey is about actively contributing to our mental health as well as realizing and accepting the complexity of our thoughts.

Being proactive in your self-care and self-empowerment is essential to taking charge of your mental health. Imagine this chapter as a road map for building resilience, encouraging good habits, and taking back control of your mental and emotional states as I walk you through it.

Being self-aware is the first step toward empowerment. We may understand the complexities of our ideas, feelings, and behavioral patterns by engaging in introspection and reflection. It's about appreciating our brains' particular landscape and accepting, without passing judgment, our strengths and weaknesses.

After gaining self-awareness, the process continues with self-care routines. I urge you to experiment with a variety of methods that suit your own requirements, be they mindfulness, meditation, physical activity, or artistic expression. These are tools that may be tailored to your interests rather than universal answers.

The idea of personal empowerment in mental health goes beyond self-care and includes developing a resilient attitude. This entails learning how to overcome obstacles, overcome failures, and adjust to the constantly shifting circumstances of life. Together, we'll investigate methods to strengthen your mental toughness that combine elements of old knowledge and modern therapy techniques.

Mental health activities not only improve your personal quality of life but also help society as a whole go in the direction of compassion and understanding.

Engaging in mental health activities is not only an individual pursuit; it is a community action that promotes empathy and understanding in society. Upon contemplating the effects of this kind of involvement, I am reminded of how closely our personal well is linked to the welfare of the larger community.

Actively participating in mental health activities has a beneficial knock-on impact. The advantages of mental health and self-care go beyond our individual lives and have an impact on the community in which we live. We set an example for people around us by putting our mental health first, dispelling stigmas and promoting candid discussions.

A culture that appreciates and gives priority to mental health is also, by nature, more caring. Empathy develops as people become aware of their own feelings and difficulties. An atmosphere of support is fostered by people's increased awareness of the subtleties of mental health, enabling them to share their experiences without fear of being judged.

Essentially, choosing to participate in mental health activities becomes a little but meaningful step toward creating a society that is more understanding and caring. It's an acknowledgment that everyone has a shared responsibility for mental health and that by encouraging an environment of transparency and encouragement, we can all help create a community that is more sympathetic and healthy.

I want you, my dear friends, to contemplate the cascading impact of your own empowerment. You may inspire others around you by prioritizing your own well-being. It is a call to action for people to start their own journeys of mental health and self-discovery.

Furthermore, the advantages apply to the group as a whole, not just to the individual. When a community as a whole adopts mental health awareness, it becomes more resilient, empathetic, and compassionate. The common language of well-being builds connections, encourages empathy, and forges a community of support where each person's path is valued and recognized.

Novel Approaches to Anxiety

The treatment of anxiety entails investigating cutting-edge strategies that go beyond conventional practices. Explore the world of cutting-edge devices and goods made especially to reduce anxiety in this area. The development of these technologies offers people new ways to control and deal with their anxiety, highlighting the intriguing relationship between technology and well-being.

One interesting case study concerns a device that resembles bubble wrap and has drawn interest due to its possible advantages in the treatment of anxiety. I hope to shed light on the design, operation, and science of this novel approach's ability to reduce anxiety as we examine its complexities. This investigation promotes a sophisticated comprehension of the ways in which unusual but useful tools might support a comprehensive strategy for mental health.

In-depth, we explore the science underlying this device's ability to reduce anxiety. This entails investigating the psychology of tactile interaction and how it affects the decrease of stress. Our mission strives to close the gap between evidence-based understanding and innovation as we explore the underlying scientific principles, promoting a nuanced view of unusual yet meaningful tools in the field of mental health.

Effective anxiety management is a journey that is not appropriate for every person. Everybody experiences anxiety differently, and there is a vast range of remedies that work for different people. By promoting receptivity to novel ideas, we recognize the wide range of instruments and methods at our disposal. The sector offers a plethora of opportunities, ranging from cutting-edge technology advancements to conventional therapy procedures.

The understanding that nontraditional methods and accepted therapy techniques may coexist is a basic component of this openness. Rather than selecting one over the other, the goal is to build a toolbox that meets the needs of each individual. This combination of methods guarantees a thorough and individualized approach to anxiety management.

Breaking free from cultural stereotypes and preconceived beliefs about non-traditional instruments is crucial to promoting openness. It's important to approach cutting-edge devices and goods with curiosity and without passing judgment. This candor enables us to recognize the possible advantages that may be found in approaches we had not previously thought about.

Furthermore, adopting new approaches necessitates constant communication between patients, mental health providers, and the general public. Educating one another with scientific discoveries, experiences, and ideas helps us all understand what works and why. The free flow of information is a driving force behind advancements in the treatment of anxiety.

One of the most effective tools we have in achieving well-being is self-reflection. It is a continuous process, a purposeful stop to recognize our feelings, ideas, and behaviors. We may better understand our triggers, resiliency, and opportunities for improvement by reflecting on ourselves. It is a self-discovery trip that is consistent with the concept of the Looking Glass, which is a gateway to a deeper understanding of oneself.

As awareness of mental health issues continues to grow, accepting change is becoming increasingly important to our overall well-being. The benefits include the expanded conversation about mental health as well as the wide range of instruments and services that are at one's disposal. Simply asking for help and using these tools is a sign of resilience and dedication to one's own development.

As we work together to combat stigmas, remove obstacles, and promote a more inclusive approach to mental health, there are many opportunities for personal development. This progress necessitates taking an active role in our own mental health and being open to trying new things. By appreciating the good things in life and the chances for improvement, we give ourselves the strength to deal with the complexity of today's mental health environment.

Remember that mental health is a journey rather than a destination and that every action we take enhances our capacity for resilience and general well-being. By means of continuous introspection and aggressive action, we may jointly mold a future in which mental health is fostered, comprehended, and honored.

Chapter 8 – The Inner Superpower

Acknowledgment and Dedication

I cannot stress enough how important it is to recognize these tender times of transition as a parent who just went through the humbling experience of accompanying my kid to graduate school. For the pupils, the start of a new school year is an exciting time full of possibilities, unrealized potential, and a sense of unease.

I send my warmest regards to the young brains entering the wide world of education, whether they are interacting in the vibrant virtual world or walking into actual classrooms. I hope that this academic journey will be full of rich experiences that encourage deep personal development in addition to intellectual advancement. I hope it turns into a journey of self-awareness, resiliency, and several academic successes.

In my experience as a Recreational Therapist, scheduled activities and interactions have the ability to change individuals. In addition to achieving academic achievement, I want kids to flourish holistically—that is, in all areas—including mental health, social skills, and a feeling of community within their learning environments. The prospect of a fresh academic year is a call to investigate, scrutinize, and seize the variety of prospects that await.

I explain the range of feelings that come with this big change in a parent's life—whether it's the first time or a recurring event—when they send their kids off to school. Acknowledging your child's progress and the milestones ahead of them requires a careful balancing act between pride, joy, and a hint of nostalgia.

It seemed like the conclusion of years of arduous effort, late-night study sessions, and the constant quest for knowledge when my child's graduation finally arrived. I felt a distinct sense of pride as we assembled for the commencement ceremony, realizing that all of the hardships and sacrifices had brought us to this momentous day.

My child's cap and gown represented not just academic success but also a life-changing process of self-discovery. Excitement crackled in the air like static, and every step leading up to the platform seemed to reverberate with the innumerable hours spent in libraries, the fortitude in the face of obstacles in the classroom, and the development that had taken place inside those university walls.

There was a tangible sense of excitement for the future, for new possibilities and frontiers. It was a bridge that united the pride of the past with the boundless possibilities of the future—a shared exhilaration.

It was hard not to think back on the path that led us to this point: the first day of school, the family meals filled with laughter, the quiet moments of support at trying times. The sentimentality served as a gentle reminder that this graduation was a new phase in the life of cherished memories rather than merely an end.

There was a subtle nervousness along with excitement as my child walked to the stage to get that well-deserved diploma. It was more of a parental apprehension about the unknown lands ahead than a questioning of their competence. The world outside of school may be exciting and intimidating at the same time, and parents' protective instincts may have raised doubts about their preparedness for the difficulties that lay ahead.

But in the middle of these feelings, a significant understanding dawned on us: our parental and child roles are always changing. The graduation signaled a change in our relationship more than simply my child's achievement.

Taking my kid to graduate school was a big parenting achievement for me. A significant event like this is accompanied by a wide range of feelings, from pride and joy to a tinge of nostalgia and maybe even anxiety. It's a journey for the students as well as for us parents, who must negotiate the difficult awareness that our kids are growing up and starting new chapters in their lives.

Being Your Own Superhero

Without capes or costumes, a superhero's true strength is found in the deep well of strength that each and every person has. That strength—the ability to face obstacles, overcome anxieties, and tenaciously pursue our goals—is something that goes beyond the magical stories seen in comic books and motion pictures and instead originates from the very essence of who we are.

If you will, see the well-known superhero flying through the air, bucking gravity and triumphing over what seems like insurmountable obstacles. Now, project that picture onto your own life. Even while the difficulties we encounter don't include supervillains or catastrophic events, they nonetheless have a big impact on our own stories. The fundamental idea is always the same, whether one is battling internal conflicts, outside pressures, or high aspirations: the need to tap into an incredible strength that is inside.

This inner strength is a real force that exists within every one of us; it is not a legendary quality reserved for fictitious characters. It's the courage that maintains our commitment in the face of fear, the determination that drives us toward self-realization, and the resilience that keeps us moving forward in the face of adversity. It's an understanding that we have the ability to control our own fate in spite of life's difficulties.

The superhero metaphor turns into a moving comparison of the difficulties people face when it comes to their mental health and personal growth. It's an admission that our struggles, even though they're not always obvious to the unaided eye, are important and life-changing. When we draw on this inner strength, we can handle everything from mundane stressors to major life transformations. This is when the superhero inside of us comes out.

Through the process of self-discovery and therapeutic intervention, I have witnessed people find their inner superheroes. The process entails removing layers to reveal special talents that could have gone undetected or latent. Realizing that one may be their own hero without having superhuman powers by embracing the underlying strengths, resilience, and coping skills developed from life events is an uplifting discovery.

Superhero Coping Skills

I have experienced the deep difficulties that come with seeing someone you care about navigate the complex terrain of worry. It's a voyage that reaches the very center of a person, particularly when there is a deep emotional bond. The challenges of helping a loved one deal with anxiety may be overwhelming since it requires a careful balancing act between empathy and the need to console the sufferer.

Let's explore the complex network of stressors, both good and negative, and how they affect the anxiety tangle. Even if they are joyful events like weddings, eustress (also known as positive stressor) like these can provide a special set of difficulties. Seeing anxiety take hold in these situations is like trying to find your way through a maelstrom of feelings in order to find the right coping strategy that would provide some respite. It serves as a reminder that worry and anxiety may arise in the human psyche even during happy situations.

On the other hand, distress (also known as negative stressor), such as the worry about having another unsuccessful marriage, have an effect that goes well beyond the current circumstance. These emotionally charged pressures can cause anxiety based on deeply ingrained fears from the past and worries about the future. Anxiety was a major strain that I experienced in my own journey—the worry of getting married again. A whirlwind of emotions that needed to be carefully navigated was brought on by the idea of sharing my life with someone else, the anxiety of making the same errors again, and the uncertainty of the future.

The concern of remarrying turned out to be a significant and complex issue. It was a time in my life when the lingering effects of the past mixed with the unpredictability of the future to create a very different emotional tapestry. Beyond the happy event that is usually associated with weddings, the choice to get into a second marriage was fraught with complications.

The dread of getting married again came from a very private place where the remnants of past relationships and the wounds they caused shadowed the possibility of fresh starts. It was a concern that spoke to the universal human experience of being vulnerable and being reluctant to let love into one's heart again.

There was a tangible emotional burden associated with the worry of yet another broken marriage. Doubts and questions mixed together to create a mental landscape where the dread of making the same mistakes again and the need for company collided. This internal conflict, which was frequently silent and introspective, necessitated a sophisticated self-awareness and a purposeful attempt to negotiate the emotional landscape.

This concern was heightened in large part by the uncertainty of the unknown. The idea of living with someone else once more, starting a future together, and taking on new obligations were daunting thoughts. Not only was there a dread of personal letdown, but there was also worry for the welfare of a prospective spouse and the effect on their lives.

Achieving a calm state of mind requires striking a careful balance between accepting the validity of worries based on the past and developing the bravery to believe that a bright future is possible. Getting help through therapy was a helpful setting to work through these complications, enabling open self-reflection and a better comprehension of the dominant worries.

In the end, overcoming this concern led to a profound process of self-discovery. In order to actively create a new story, it required removing the layers of fear, facing the ghosts of the past, and building a sense of empowerment. It was evidence of the human spirit's tenacity—its capacity to face uncertainties, draw lessons from the past, and start over with bravery and optimism.

Taking Risks and Overcoming Anxiety

Anxiety-induced inclination to shy away from positive stimuli reveals a nuanced relationship between the human mind and the expectation of happy occasions. It's a phenomenon where the entire idea of something good, like getting married, going on an exciting trip, or starting a new chapter, becomes tied up in a web of anxiety and discomfort. To grasp and maneuver this complex dance, one must explore the subtle facets of anxiety and how it affects how we perceive eustress. Fundamentally, this avoidance stems from a fear reaction—a fear of what is unknown, a fear of becoming helpless, or maybe a fear of the changes that eustress could bring about in our lives. The mind might interpret stresses as possible dangers, leading to a chain reaction of uneasy thoughts and feelings, even if they are essentially happy and promising.

This avoidance is mostly driven by a fear of the unknown. It might be intimidating to venture into unfamiliar terrain, especially if it holds the promise of happiness and fulfillment. Eustress may be seen by the mind, which is hardwired to seek familiarity and predictability, as changes to the status quo can cause unease and hesitancy.

The absence of control emerges as another important element. Eustress sometimes include circumstances that are beyond our direct control, and giving up control can be unsettling. Eustress may be anything from the uncertainty of starting a new relationship to the difficulties of changing careers or organizing a big event; whatever the stressor, the mind fights the sense of being in the dark and intensifies the anxiety.

This avoidance is further compounded by the worry that success and constructive change may upset the current balance. There's a comfort in the known, and the idea of favorable stresses upsetting this balance might make people reluctant to accept change. It's as if the mind blocks its own natural aspirations for happiness and development in an effort to protect itself from any suffering.

Uncovering these anxieties and narratives consciously is necessary to overcome the inclination to shy away from good stresses. It requires acknowledging that eustress is an essential component of life, just like distress. You may change your viewpoint by accepting the unknown, owning your fear, and reinterpreting these pressures as chances for personal development.

Self-discovery is the path toward overcoming the avoidance of eustress. It entails confronting the myths that prevent us from moving forward, developing resilience in the face of uncertainty, and giving ourselves permission to enjoy the richness of life's worthwhile challenges without being constrained by needless fear.

Anxiety may cause immobility and stagnation, which is a difficult problem that frequently includes a complex interaction of behavioral, emotional, and psychological elements. It's a condition where worry strengthens its grasp, making it difficult to go forward and entangling people in a vicious cycle of fear and inaction. We must investigate the underlying roots of these worries and consider escape routes from this paralyzing cycle if we are to empower people to evaluate and face their anxieties.

- **Fear of Failure:**

The fear of failing is a common cause of immobility. Anxiety frequently exaggerates the possible negative effects of failure, erecting a mental barrier that keeps people from taking chances. The mind may exaggerate the possible bad outcomes in an effort to defend itself from imagined hazards, which can result in a crippling anxiety of making the incorrect decision.

- **Perfectionism:**

Perfectionism has the potential to be a covert saboteur that causes immobility. A feeling of inadequacy can be cultivated by the need for faultless results and the anxiety associated with not meeting expectations. People might become immobilized by this dread of falling short of unachievably high standards, which keeps them from acting unless everything is just right.

- **Overestimation of Risk:**

Anxiety frequently warps perceptions of risk, making things seem more dangerous than they actually are. People tend to overestimate the possibility of bad things happening, which makes them feel more dangerous. They may get immobilized as a result of this overestimation because they weigh the possible hazards against the advantages of taking a chance.

- **Comfort in the Familiar:**

A sense of security comes from familiarity, and the unease that comes with the unknown can be heightened by anxiousness. Even when it keeps one in a place where things are stagnating, the fear of moving outside one's comfort zone may be a strong motivator. In an attempt to protect itself, the mind opposes change and keeps people stuck in the familiar, even when it isn't satisfying.

Encouraging people to evaluate and face their concerns requires a calculated and caring approach:

- **Mindful Self-Reflection:**

People are urged to practice attentive introspection in order to pinpoint the precise worries that keep them from moving. This entails accepting ideas and emotions without passing judgment. Destroying the power of anxiety requires first understanding its origins.

- **Redefining Failure:**

It's critical to change how failure is seen. Reframing failure as a necessary component of learning and development might help people rethink how they view setbacks. It is empowering to promote a mindset that sees failure as a learning opportunity rather than an insurmountable barrier.

- **Gradual Exposure:**

Systematic desensitization—also referred to as gradual exposure to the dreaded situations—can be a useful tactic. This entails making gradual, controlled progress toward the desired result. Every step that is effective increases self-assurance and loosens anxiety's hold.

- **Setting Realistic Goals:**

The intimidating quality of more significant jobs is diminished when people are encouraged to set reasonable, attainable goals. A step-by-step method is made possible by breaking goals down into smaller, more manageable components, which lessens the intimidating nature of progress.

- **Cultivating a Growth Mindset:**

Developing a development mindset is realizing that aptitude and intellect may be enhanced with commitment and diligence. This kind of thinking builds resilience in the face of failure by encouraging people to see obstacles as chances for personal development.

People can start to emerge from immobility by addressing these underlying worries and learning techniques for progressive confrontation. This approach, my dear friend, entails not only confronting anxieties head-on but also cultivating an outlook that sees setbacks as opportunities for growth and fulfillment on a personal level.

Embrace the Hero Within

In my own path, I had to face a powerful foe: my second marriage's anxiety and panic attacks. The anxiety of starting this new chapter in my life turned into a turbulent undercurrent that threatened to ruin the happy occasion of marriage. This incredibly intimate tale highlights the value of resiliency and the life-changing effects of getting expert assistance to escape the bonds that bind us.

- **Facing the Fear of Another Failed Marriage:**

Anxiety surfaced as a dominant force in the mixture of emotions triggered by the possibility of getting married again. Slight worries about the difficulties of living together and starting a family again were exacerbated by the possibility that history may repeat itself. Despite being reasonable, the echoes of prior events took on a life of their own and transformed into a crippling worry that threatened to overwhelm the joyful anticipation of a wedding.

Like a master illusionist, the fear accentuated the difficulties of a second marriage, making them seem more difficult than they actually were. Commonplace issues like living together and making decisions together were overshadowed by previous setbacks and turned into insurmountable barriers in the mind's environment. What ought to have been a time of joy and celebration turned into a weak match where the dread of failing was very real.

The generally joyful times of getting ready for the wedding were clouded with uncertainty and fear due to this fear. It was challenging to manage the dissonance that resulted from the good stressor of wedding planning being eclipsed by the distress of worry and uncertainty. The difficulty lay not just in dealing with the pragmatics of marriage but also in breaking down the psychological walls worry had built.

It's critical to recognize that these worries were legitimate and based on real experiences. The emotional burden of former relationships adds layers to the already intricate complexity of combining two lives. But anxiety's tendency to magnify things warped these worries, making them seem like powerful enemies. A powerful enemy that threatened to sabotage the possibility of a fresh chapter emerged: the worry that history might repeat itself.

- **Experiencing a Panic Attack:**

What ought to have been a period of excitement and optimism instead found me in the confusing grasp of a panic attack. For a brief time, the tangible excitement that usually accompanies wedding planning was eclipsed by a powerful, visceral feeling that appeared to arise from the core of my own fears.

The scenario was very paradoxical: the happy stressor of wedding preparation, which is normally connected to joy and celebration, clashed with the distress of worry and anxiety. It was a collision of feelings that highlighted the delicate dance between happiness and fear, illustrating how difficult it is to navigate life's milestones when worry stalks you.

The physical and psychological signs of a panic attack were unwaveringly intense during this event. My heart was thumping so fast, I was shaking, and my throat was constricted; all of these emotions overshadowed the happy times for a little while. It seemed as though the anxiety that had been suppressed during the times of organizing and getting ready had now found a way to surface and make itself known.

Following the panic attack, there was a strong feeling of detachment. For a little while, the eustress of wedding planning—which ought to have served as a uniting factor—felt disconnected from the bad stressor of worry. It served as a sobering reminder that anxiety's shadow may remain for a long time and cause disruption, even during happy times.

- **Two Choices: Self-Sabotage or Seeking Help:**

Faced with the inner turmoil caused by worry, I discovered that I was at a crucial juncture where I had to choose between two options. Self-sabotage was the first route, which was maybe the simpler but more harmful one. This would entail giving in to the anxiety's powerful pull and letting it slowly undermine the basis of the developing connection. Taking the second route, which was more difficult but ultimately transforming, involved facing my worries head-on with the important assistance of a mental health specialist.

Choosing the latter signified a deliberate choice to get assistance instead of giving in to the debilitating consequences of worry. I came to see that getting through the complex web of fears required more than just my own willpower; it also required the knowledge and understanding of a licensed therapist. By seeking professional assistance, I embarked on a self-exploration and resilience journey, establishing the foundation for a stronger and more robust approach to the difficulties that lie ahead.

- **Therapeutic Intervention:**

Starting a therapeutic intervention journey was a crucial step in my search to comprehend and get over the complexities of my concerns and anxieties. Through its transforming power, therapy offered a secure and encouraging environment where I could have an honest conversation and explore the depths of my emotional terrain.

The therapy procedure included a thorough investigation of the underlying causes of my apprehensions in addition to analyzing the outward signs of worry. I worked with my therapist to identify the causes of these worries, figuring out how my relationships' particular dynamics, personal narratives, and prior experiences all interacted.

I learned a great deal about the patterns that fed my fears, thanks to the therapy process. This comprehension served as the basis for the development of customized therapies. The individualized tactics, developed in conjunction with my therapist, were intended to target particular triggers, mental patterns, and emotional reactions.

As the therapy process progressed, I acquired a plethora of coping skills that enabled me to traverse the emotional terrain with enhanced resilience. Through cognitive reframing that challenged harmful thinking patterns and mindfulness practices that kept me grounded in the present, therapy gave me useful tools to face and manage my worries.

- **The Result: A Resilient 16-Year Marriage:**

Looking back at the sixteen years that have passed since I faced the anxiety related to my second marriage, I can clearly see how important it was to choose therapy intervention in order to support not just the survival of my marriage but also my own development and fortitude. What at first appeared to be an insurmountable obstacle became a chance for deep self-reflection and fortitude.

Being my own superhero meant releasing myself from the bonds of anxiety. The recognition of one's own limitations and the steadfast will to overcome them constituted the fundamental aspects of this voyage. Seeking expert assistance was not a show of weakness but rather a calculated action, similar to recruiting a supporter on the road to one's own triumph.

The therapist role became apparent as a stabilizing influence, proving essential in helping me navigate the maze of fears and make the breakthrough. This emphasizes a vital component of becoming a superhero: realizing that even those with superhuman power need teammates and support networks. In this situation, I was helping others and myself by providing techniques, understanding, and a safe environment for self-discovery.

Empowering Others: Inspiring Positive Change

I've come across real-life instances that demonstrate people's extraordinary perseverance in the face of mental health difficulties. One such story is about a brave college student who fights anxiety and panic attacks; it highlights the challenges, but, more significantly, it celebrates the moments of empowerment.

The student desperately begged not to go during the panic episode, saying, almost in a panic, "I can't go, please believe me, I can't do it on my own." I'm not going." The student used the panic attack as a therapeutic way to communicate their deep dread of the unknown and the major life shift they were going to undergo during this vulnerable period.

But what really makes this narrative beautiful isn't the panic attack per se; rather, it's what happened next. The student started working through the procedures required to deal with their concerns and social anxiety as the anxiety storm passed, equipped with a clearer perspective. It's evidence of one's inner fortitude, courage to face fear head-on, and the need to ask for support and assistance.

The students had to deal with adjusting to a new environment, making new friends, and figuring out the nuances of college life as they started their trip. Even with that first panic episode, there was a slow but noticeable change over the next few weeks and months. Although the student's worry persisted, they were able to navigate and control it, showing a great level of empowerment.

Supporting Others and Seeking Help

This true story emphasizes how important it is to identify and honor superhero moments—the times when people overcome fear by taking courageous action that empowers them. The path could entail getting expert assistance, as this student did in later years, to be ready for graduate school, or it might entail learning coping strategies and coping mechanisms to deal with life's challenges.

Undoubtedly, sending a child off to college is a significant event that elicits a range of feelings, including pride, enthusiasm, nostalgia, and maybe even a little bit of anxiety. Support networks play a critical role in these situations, especially for parents.

I offer my sympathies and support to all the parents who are negotiating the difficult yet exciting reality that their children are growing up and starting new chapters in their lives. We are on a trip just as much as they are. It's normal to experience a range of emotions as we see our kids make those moves toward independence. Experiencing both satisfaction in their achievements and the slight melancholy that comes with their leaving is acceptable.

Building a strong support network and relying on it during these changes is crucial. Having a network to share these feelings with may be comforting, whether it is by interacting with other parents going through the same situations, joining community groups, or finding comfort in close friends. It's a chance to share knowledge and counsel and, above all, to let yourself know that you're not the only one going through this significant transition.

Furthermore, I want to stress how critical it is to eradicate the stigma attached to getting treatment. Insofar as I have personally experienced the transformational potential of therapy, I think that empowering parents and people to get professional assistance is essential to achieving holistic well-being. A secure place to work with the complexities of our worries, concerns, and the range of emotions that come with big life changes is provided by therapy.

There is sometimes an unjustified stigma in our culture around therapy—a false belief that it is exclusively for persons with serious mental health issues. Therapy, however, may be an effective instrument for negotiating life's complexity and for personal growth and self-discovery. By removing these obstacles and encouraging transparency, we enable people to place a higher priority on their mental health.

The benefits of professional assistance while dealing with mental health issues as well as when taking proactive measures to better oneself. It's a way to build resilience overall, acquire perspective, and create coping methods. The well-being of our children is inextricably linked to our own as parents. We have a good impact on others around us when we look after our mental health as well as ourselves.

Identifying Symptoms of Panic Attacks

The Mayo Clinic lists a number of symptoms, and it's crucial to remember that people may have a mix of them while they're having a panic attack. A sense of impending doom or danger, fear of losing control or dying, a fast beating heart, sweating, trembling, shaking, chills, hot flashes, nausea, abdominal cramps, headache, dizziness, lightheadedness, fainting, numbness, tingling sensations, and feelings of detachment or unreality are some of these symptoms.

The sensation is visceral and overpowering because of the fast-beating heart rate and the fear of impending doom that goes along with it. In addition to the physical symptoms, trembling and sweating produce a complicated mixture of feelings that can be difficult to process. Breathlessness and constriction in the throat exacerbate the feeling of being overpowered.

It's important to underscore that the contrast between the distress of dread and anxiety and the eustress that triggers the attack, like the excitement of a wedding, emphasizes how complicated these emotions are. Even in circumstances that ought to make one happy or joyful, panic episodes frequently strike without warning.

I've learned to stop and take deep breaths whenever I feel that quickening heartbeat or constriction in my throat. Exercises that include deep breathing make me feel peaceful and in control of my breathing. Furthermore, grounding strategies, including paying attention to my local environment or concentrating on something, have worked well for me in refocusing my attention from overpowering feelings.

Beyond the costumes and capes, it's about realizing that we have the incredible capacity to face our fears, conquer obstacles, and follow our objectives with unwavering determination. I urge you to consider their own goals and interests. Which dreams are you keeping hidden because you're afraid or anxious? It's time to accept your inner superhero and take measured chances. No matter how big or little, these risks help us grow as individuals and present chances to release the bonds that bind us.

Chapter 9 - Reinvent Your Brave Soul

Embracing the Reality of Life's Uncertainties

Let us first embrace the fundamental reality that life happens — sometimes with unexpected energy, sometimes with soft whispers — as we embark on this journey together, my friend. We must give ourselves breaks from time to time in the middle of these ups and downs, the tides of life.

The environment we live in demands our attention and draws us in a variety of ways. Yet, we frequently forget how important it is to take care of our own well-being in the clamor of responsibilities and expectations. It's at these times of turmoil and upheaval that self-care becomes especially important.

So I'm extending you an invite, my dear friend: in the middle of all the difficulties in life, take a moment to stop, think, and put yourself first because it is in these peaceful times that we discover comfort, clarity, and the willpower to endure.

We will delve into the nuances of reinvention on this journey, which is both profound and intimate. Let's go together to the core of our dreams, overcoming obstacles caused by fear and self-doubt along the way. But do not be alarmed; uncertainty really presents a chance for development and change.

Reinventing Yourself: What Does It Mean?

Let's explore the notion of reinvention and highlight its

complexity. Reinvention is the essence of regeneration and transformation in both personal and professional spheres. It represents a purposeful change in course, an intentional attempt to remake oneself in the service of development and fulfillment.

Reinvention in the personal realm is a process of self-realization and self-discovery that goes beyond simple change. It entails dissecting our identities, challenging ingrained convictions, and accepting the fluidity of our changing identities. It involves reflecting on ourselves and facing our vulnerabilities, hopes, and anxieties head-on with unshakable bravery.

Likewise, in the workplace, reinvention takes the form of a calculated effort to adjust to and prosper in a constantly shifting environment. Seeking professional contentment requires a willingness to question the current quo, investigate novel approaches, and welcome innovation. It is evidence of our adaptability and resiliency as we negotiate the challenges of changing careers and advancing professionally.

Understanding that change and growth are inevitable is essential to the reinvention notion. Flux and fluxion are characteristics of life by definition. Our experiences—both the good and the bad—all weave together to form the fabric of our identities, both personal and professional. These events help us develop resilience, gain fresh perspectives, and pave new paths.

Reinvention also requires an understanding of how one's objectives and sense of self are always changing. Our goals, objectives, and wants change throughout time as a result of the dynamic interaction between our values, interests, and experiences in life. Because of this, the process of reinvention necessitates a readiness to accept change, explore uncharted territory, and redefine success according to our own standards.

Redefining who you are ultimately proves the strength of the human spirit and our ability to evolve, adapt, and learn about ourselves. It's a voyage full of unknowns and difficulties, but it's also full of endless opportunities. Therefore, you must embrace this path of transformation with bravery, conviction, and unflinching commitment and set out on it with open hearts and minds.

Evolving Nature of Personal Identity and Goals

Understanding the reinvention process requires acknowledging the dynamic nature of personal identity and objectives. As we traverse the intricacies of life, our personal identity is dynamic and prone to change. Our experiences, values, and sense of self are shaped by the new chances, difficulties, and encounters we have while moving through various stages and phases.

A strong sense of self-awareness—a continuous investigation of our identities, beliefs, and goals—lays the foundation of personal identity. Moments of self-discovery throughout this reflective process allow us to face our anxieties and insecurities, reveal previously undiscovered aspects of our personalities, and develop a more profound awareness of our true selves.

Furthermore, as we develop as individuals, so do our ambitions and aims. As we become more aware of our beliefs, interests, and priorities, something that formerly appeared as a far-off dream or hope may transform into a real objective. Alternatively, when we experience personal development and metamorphosis, objectives that were meaningful to us in the past could no longer be relevant.

The dynamic character of the human experience is reflected in the way that personal identity and objectives change throughout time. It is evidence of our ability to develop, adapt, and persevere in the face of changes and obstacles in life. Accepting this progress necessitates being open to new ideas and viewpoints, willing to accept change, and willing to question preconceived beliefs.

A strong foundation for traveling this path of self-discovery and development is offered by reinvention. It gives us the ability to rewrite our own story, forge new directions, and live lives that are consistent with our most cherished goals and beliefs. We welcome the fluidity of the human experience by accepting the fact that personal identity and aspirations change throughout time. We also recognize that change may be a driver for personal growth and satisfaction.

Concrete Steps to Reinvention:

A. Reflecting on One's Own Goals and Desires:

Reflecting deeply and honestly on our individual goals, beliefs, and wants is the first step toward reinvention. It necessitates finding peaceful times in the midst of the bustle of everyday existence so that we can explore the depths of our hearts and thoughts.

I challenge your boldness to pose meaningful questions to yourself throughout this introspective process: What makes me happy and fulfilled? Which hobbies and passions are the deepest for me? What principles do I uphold, and how do they influence my ambitions and goals? We may obtain important insights into our true selves by honestly and openly exploring these topics, which paves the way for significant reinvention.

B. Making a Wish List to Grow Both Professionally and Personally:

The next stage is to turn our personal aims and wants into concrete goals and objectives after we have obtained clarity on them. I'd like to extend an invitation to you to start a wishful thinking trip. Imagine the life you want to live, both personally and professionally, and put these goals into words that you can put on a tangible wish list.

This wish list covers a wide range of goals, from daring endeavors to career milestones, and acts as a road map for both professional and personal development. Every item on the wish list serves as a beacon of hope and promise, pointing us in the direction of our aspirations, whether they are related to developing new skills, going on a journey, or growing in your job.

C. Determining Neglected Objectives and Proactively Pursuing Them:

Throughout our lives, we often come across ambitions that have been put off because of external factors or constraints that we put on ourselves. It is imperative that we recognize these neglected objectives as we set out on the reinvention journey and take deliberate measures to make them a reality.

This calls for a readiness to face our anxieties and worries, to question the status quo, and to cast off the chains of complacency. Every objective that is put off, whether it is going back to school, taking care of neglected relationships, or looking into new employment options, is a chance for development and change.

By taking deliberate and proactive steps towards these postponed goals, we reclaim agency over our lives, infusing them with purpose, passion, and meaning. It is through these courageous acts of self-discovery and self-realization that we forge new pathways forward, embracing the boundless potential that resides within us.

Overcoming Resistance and Self-Doubt:

A. Identifying Self-doubt and Reluctance to Change:

I inevitably encountered opposition to change and struggled with self-doubt on my path to reinvention. These inner conflicts frequently showed up as a persistent lack of confidence in the future, a fear of exploring the unknown, and a reluctance to move outside of my comfort zone.

As I worked through these difficult feelings, I realized that admitting and recognizing them was the first vital step. It meant facing my inner demons, illuminating the dark corners of my psyche, and accepting vulnerability as a driving force behind development and self-awareness.

I discovered that by embracing these unpleasant feelings, I could start to remove the barriers and self-doubt preventing me from moving forward. It was an introspective and self-examination process that required bravery and honesty as I delved more into my feelings and ideas. I came to view resistance and self-doubt as allies rather than enemies on my path despite the discomfort. They acted as markers, pointing me in the direction of my own development and evolution. I was also reminded of my innate resilience and tenacity as I made my way through them.

I learned to accept the unknowns and difficulties that came with reinventing myself with every step I took. It was a path of self-awareness and personal development, driven by a readiness to face my anxieties and welcome the opportunities that lay beyond my comfort zone. Through it all, I learned the value of vulnerability as a means of achieving contentment and authenticity.

B. Promoting Taking Chances and Venturing Beyond Your Comfort Zones:

I urge you, my friend, to embrace risk-taking and bravely venture outside of your comfort zone in the face of resistance and self-doubt. True development and transformation occur when we push ourselves to face the unknown and go beyond our preconceived boundaries, which is where discomfort and uncertainty thrive.

Accept the strange, the unknown, and the uncharted, for it is in these places that the seeds of reinvention are planted. Every action we take to venture beyond our comfort zone, whether it is by seizing new chances, venturing into uncharted territory, or accepting unique experiences, acts as a catalyst for our own personal development and self-discovery.

C. Stressing the Value of Endurance and Patience in the Process of Reinvention:

There are obstacles and failures on the path of reinvention. As we negotiate the complexity of change and transition, the path is full of turns and twists, highs and lows. Perseverance and patience become guiding qualities in the face of hardship, shedding resilience and fortitude on the journey ahead.

Accept the path with steadfast resolve, understanding that obstacles are actually opportunities for personal development and self-discovery. As you move through the ups and downs of the reinvention process, practice patience and have faith in the innate wisdom of your experience and the transformational potential of tenacity.

Organic Reinvention: Allowing Change to Happen

A. Exploring How Life Experiences Can Naturally Lead to Reinvention:

Life is a journey with ups and downs, successes and setbacks, and every event helps to shape and mold us into the people we are today. The natural evolution that takes place while we negotiate the highs and lows of life's many experiences is known as organic reinvention. It's the act of welcoming the chances for personal development and evolution that present themselves along the road and letting change happen naturally, free from coercion or manipulation.

We start to realize how profoundly our life experiences have shaped our views, values, and goals when we think back on them. Every event, no matter how big or little, acts as a catalyst for personal development and change. It provides priceless lessons and new perspectives that help us on our path to self-awareness.

B. Organic Reinvention During The Pandemic

The global chaos that accompanied the pandemic was unlike

anything we had ever seen. Many of us were left feeling scared, alone, and extremely confused about the future as lockdowns were implemented, companies closed, and everyday routines were upset. Amid all of this chaos, I, too, was faced with the frightening truth of a world in transition and had no idea what was ahead.

There was one bright spot among the mayhem: a priceless chance for reflection and self-discovery. Due to the restrictions of quarantine, I was forced to live alone and had plenty of time and space to explore the dark corners of my own mind and face the facts that were hidden from view.

I started a self-reflection journey in the peace and quiet of my own house, removing social pressures and layers of training to find my actual self. I went to the core of my fears, hopes, and wishes and faced the unvarnished truths that had been long hidden by the diversions and cacophony of daily existence.

My life took a drastic turn for the worst at this time of deep reflection when I had a seismic awakening that would change my course forever. During the pandemic, I felt a deep-seated desire to embrace the limitless potential that was dormant inside me and to break free from the constraints of convention.

The inspiration blazed brighter and brighter every day, sparking a spark of creativity and ingenuity that had been dormant inside me for a long time. I discovered secret skills and abilities that I had never dared to explore as I dug deeper into my hobbies and interests; each discovery was a glimmer of promise and optimism amid the shadow of uncertainty.

In the middle of the pandemic's mayhem, I found myself going through a deep process of reinvention—a voyage of self-awareness and empowerment that would eventually inspire me to seize fresh chances, pave new routes, and rethink the core of who I was always intended to be.

I came out of the crisis crucible not as a victim of my circumstances but as a resilient person, able to withstand hardship and come out stronger, smarter, and more capable than before. Even though the path ahead may be paved with obstacles and unknowns, I am walking it with a renewed sense of purpose and resolve, confident that I possess the ability to transcend, change, and succeed in the face of overwhelming adversity.

C. Accepting Unforeseen Chances for Personal Development and Exploration:

Accepting the unanticipated chances for development and self-discovery that present themselves amid life's hardships is the essence of organic reinvention. It involves submitting to the innate knowledge of the cosmos, believing in the ability of change to bring about transformation, and letting the currents of fate lead us.

We expose ourselves to new options and routes that are outside of our comfort zones when we welcome unforeseen chances for personal development. By accepting the unknown, we may reach our greatest potential and draw on reserves of inner strength, creativity, and resilience that enable us to go beyond our boundaries and reach new levels of fulfillment and purpose.

Sharing and Connecting Through Reinvention

A. Highlighting the Therapeutic Benefits of Sharing Personal Experiences

It becomes more and more clear as we go through the reinvention process that talking about our own experiences may be incredibly healing and transforming. By being honest about our own setbacks, victories, and development moments, we not only better understand ourselves but also create profound relationships with those who could be traveling down a similar route.

Talking about one's experiences may be a highly effective way to promote healing and self-discovery. By expressing our ideas, feelings, and insights, we provide people a space to be seen, heard, and understood, in addition to validating our own experiences. We dismantle barriers to isolation and foster a sense of empathy and solidarity among our communities by sharing our struggles and victories.

B. Engage and Share Your Own Reinvention Journeys

It becomes more and more clear as we go through the reinvention process that talking about our own experiences may be incredibly healing and transforming. By being honest about our own setbacks, victories, and development moments, we not only better understand ourselves but also create profound relationships with those who could be traveling down a similar route.

Talking about one's experiences may be a highly effective way to promote healing and self-discovery. By expressing our ideas, feelings, and insights, we provide people a space to be seen, heard, and understood, in addition to validating our own experiences. We dismantle barriers to isolation and foster a sense of empathy and solidarity among our communities by sharing our struggles and victories.

I am always motivated to remake myself by the tales of bravery, resiliency, and metamorphosis that I hear from other people. Every story serves as a reminder of the human spirit's innate resiliency and tenacity, as well as the limitless capacity each of us possesses to rise above hardship and seize new opportunities.

I want to encourage a sense of connection and community among us by encouraging listeners to participate and discuss their own reinvention adventures. We can all benefit from one another's knowledge, find strength in our common experiences, and recommit ourselves to our own pathways of reinvention by establishing a secure and encouraging environment for discussion and introspection.

As friends, we can successfully negotiate life's curves while acknowledging and appreciating our successes, helping one another through difficulties, and relishing the countless opportunities that lie ahead. We may develop a sense of empowerment and belonging by embracing the power of community and connection, which helps us advance in our pursuit of both professional and personal development.

Together, let's go on this road of reinvention. I encourage you to share your views, stories, and ideas with me and each other. Let's honor the wonder of our common humanity and the transforming force of connection, bravery, and resiliency. We may encourage and inspire each other, as well as set out on an endless path of self-discovery and empowerment when we work together.

Reflecting on the Transformative Power of Reinvention

The immense power that comes with accepting change and pursuing personal development really gets to me. We have explored the depths of self-discovery, confronted our preconceptions, and ventured to imagine new possibilities for ourselves and our futures during our conversation.

As we consider the transforming potential of reinvention, we are reminded of the extraordinary resiliency of the human spirit. We are capable of adapting to the ups and downs of life's journey and coming out stronger and more resilient than before. We may uncover our own inner reserves of bravery, resiliency, and promise via the process of reinvention, which also opens the way to a purposeful and exciting future.

With great conviction and optimism, I challenge each one of you to welcome change and seek personal development. Because the quest for reinvention offers the chance to escape the bonds of mediocrity and complacency and venture fearlessly into the uncharted territory of potential and transformation. We start a limitless path of self-discovery and empowerment when we embrace change and allow ourselves to be open to new possibilities, viewpoints, and horizons.

I want to end by saying how grateful I am to have had the chance to share and grow with every one of you. Our journey together has had an incredible influence on my own development and understanding. We build a feeling of community and connection and create deep connections that cut beyond time and location by the sharing of ideas, experiences, and insights. I am incredibly appreciative of the chance to accompany each of you on this path of self-revelation and to observe the strength and beauty of the human soul.

I want to encourage you, my dear readers, to embrace the transformational power of reinvention and to dare to dream big and unashamedly as we stand on the cusp of fresh beginnings and limitless possibilities. The secret to realizing the boundless potential that each of us possesses is found in the quest for personal development and self-discovery. Together, let's set off on an endless adventure of reinvention and design a route for a future full of bravery, passion, and purpose.

Chapter 10 – The Evolution Diaries

Symbolism of Goddesses and Gods

The core of accepting the goddess and god symbolism is a potent metaphor for our path to empowerment and self-discovery. We frequently go to the divine for inspiration, taking courage from the archetypal characters who stand for tenacity, discernment, and grace. Whether they are gods or goddesses, these mythical beings stand in for the eternal soul that is inside each of us.

This chapter is a study of the powerful influence these symbols have on our pursuit of personal development, drawing connections between their eternal features and our unique journeys. The archetypal characters turn into mirrors that reflect the elegance we want to embody, the power we possess, and the knowledge we desire.

So, dear friend, let's embark on a journey together to discover how you can become a powerful and self-empowered individual. Through my personal evolution, I hope to inspire you to recognize the potential within yourself to become your own Goddess or God.

Empowerment in the Midst of Challenging Times

Investigating our inner selves serves as an anchor during trying times when uncertainty reigns and the world is undergoing significant changes. Making the deliberate decision to draw from our inner source of empowerment and strength enables us to deal with life's challenges with poise and purpose.

Masks: A Unique Expression to Masks of Self-expression

Wearing masks during the heaviest time of the pandemic became a form of self-expression. The mask covered up our most important form of self-expression, our mouths. It was so much harder to read a person with the mask covering their mouth. I loved the way many of us rallied under these circumstances and began to use the mask itself as a form of self-expression.

As for myself, I loved wearing my mask that represented my Alma Mater the University of Florida. It was orange and blue, with pictures of the Gator logo all over it. People used masks to convey political statements and art as well. The downfall to the mask was that people also used it as a shield to protect and hide under.

Many felt this covered them up from really being seen by others socially, emotionally and isolating them from others by hiding behind the mask. Thankfully, the mask is behind us and so is the pandemic. Becoming a God or Goddess is about embracing the true you and empowering yourself to be true to who you are. It's time to take off the metaphorical mask that you might be hiding behind and gain confidence and power within to become your own God or Goddess.

To maximize the use of a necessary but unpleasant thing, I've expanded my selection of masks. I've enjoyed giving this essential item a little flare with everything from funny patterns to imitation designer masks. One of my faves, in honor of my rescue dog, says "Peace Love Rescue" with pride. And as a tribute to the amazing Ruth Bader Ginsburg, I have a mask made of her face, a symbol of fortitude and resiliency.

Well my dear friend, while we may never fully get used to the discomfort, why not infuse a bit of personal flair into this daily routine? Whether making a fashion statement or subtly sharing a part of yourself, embracing the mask can transform it from a simple necessity into a sign of self-expression.

Evolution Through Ages

- **20s: Uninhibited Discovery and Ambitious Beginnings**

Reaching my 20s seemed like an uninhibited discovery and the start of an ambitious journey. I was blissfully unaware of the possible repercussions of my conduct throughout this era. I was free to go with the flow, live in the now, and not bother myself with an excessive amount of future analysis at that point in time. Life was like an open book.

My first job became my official introduction to the professional world, and it was an exciting time to begin defining my goals and identity. The world was waiting to be colored by my investigation, and I embraced the opportunities and difficulties that were in front of me.

- **30s: Establishing Roots, Building a Career, and Entering Parenthood**

My transition into my 30s was more than just a change in years; it was a time of deep introspection and deliberate action. Now, the haphazard ambitions of my 20s were coming together to form specific objectives that would influence my career and personal path.

In terms of my career, I was actively laying the groundwork rather than just working. My aspirations were deliberately positioned in the professional environment. During this period, I made conscious decisions about my profession with every step I took toward achieving my goals.

Parenthood concurrently introduced a new dimension to this stage of development. A stronger feeling of purpose and a clearer focus on what was really important were brought about by the duties of raising a new life. Recalibrating priorities and fine-tuning my definition of success was necessary to strike a balance between my work aspirations and the delights and difficulties of motherhood.

During this era, establishing roots went beyond geographical locations and professional achievements to include the foundations of my identity. The challenges of establishing a job and being a mother were forming who I was becoming at the same time.

- **40s: Getting to Know Oneself and Questioning Life's Deeper Meaning**

A sense of completion and validation for the journey so far was experienced when certain goals were accomplished during this period. But even in the middle of these successes, there was a faint sense of something being in the way, something I wasn't sure I wanted to investigate completely. I was struggling with anxiety at the time and realized I had to face the challenge of moving outside of my comfortable comfort zone.

Something pulled at the corners of my mind, the yearning to change and move on to the next phase of my life. I longed to discover the inner fortitude needed for this next stage of my development. Thus, the 40s were more than simply a decade; they were a deep dive into my identity, a period in which I faced my fears and looked for the bravery to face what was ahead.

- **50s: Finding Enlightenment, Acknowledging Constant Change, and Blossoming**

A deep sense of enlightenment has come with turning fifty, a knowledge that has expanded the palette of my viewpoint. Seeing that change is inevitable has come to be seen as a guiding concept. These crucial ten years seem to be flowering, an understanding that life is a complex dance of ongoing development and adaptation.

The hard edges of my childhood have vanished to be replaced with a more adaptable acceptance of life's constant change. I've learned to appreciate the beauty in life's ups and downs throughout this time, realizing that every second counts in the continuous development of who I am. The idea of 'blossoming' captures the spirit of this phase— a deep realization that, like a flower, I am always opening up and showing new sides to myself.

I've found a certain liberty in accepting the flux of life's changes. Knowing that adaptation is a celebration of the complex waltz between stability and development rather than a capitulation has a certain elegance to it. This path of self-discovery has resulted in acceptance as well as a deep appreciation for the ongoing change.

- **Reflection on the Unique Evolution of Each Stage**

When I think back on this special development over the years, I see how each phase has added different hues to my existence.

Aspirations and adventure characterized the 20s, roots were established in the 30s, self-discovery and questioning characterized the 40s, and enlightenment and acceptance of change characterized the 50s. Every stage, with all of its difficulties and successes, has been vital in molding me into the person I am today. Looking back, I can see that my life has been composed of resilient blocks, blocks of progress, and blocks of an unrelenting determination to improve myself.

Embracing Change and Growth

A big episode in my life has begun as I approach my 50s, a time of profound transformation and a deliberate acceptance of change and development. This time has become more than just a historical turning point; it is a deep voyage of introspection and deliberate story construction.

The idea of growth and transformation has evolved from being seen as a passive event to a purposeful, deliberate choice. It is now a conscious choice to interact with the changing character of existence rather than just a result of time passing. Understanding that staying the same goes against life's natural energy, I've chosen to embrace change as a necessary component of my own development.

I now realize that our stories are things we actively create rather than ones that are prewritten. Thus, accepting change and progress is a proactive choice that will help me design the next chapters of my life rather than a reactive one. I can now take control of my story and give it meaning, resiliency, and a dedication to ongoing self-improvement because of my deliberate decision.

In order to transform in the 50s, striking a balance between cultivating an open-minded perspective and accepting the knowledge that has accumulated over time. It is appreciating the depth of experience while keeping an open mind to the unknown that change may bring. This intense dance is now a source of great joy as well as difficulty.

My viewpoint has changed as a result of the 50s, and I now see change as an opportunity for emotional and personal development rather than as a danger. Every turn in life's path is a chance for growth in self-awareness, resilience, and learning. Putting progress first has become a pillar that directs choices, deeds, and the general course of my changing story.

- **Shifting Perspective on Oneself:**

I no longer see myself through the same lens that I once did. My youthful fears no longer limit me; instead, I've adopted a more sympathetic and perceptive outlook. It's about accepting oneself with all of its flaws and realizing that the path of self-discovery never ends. This change has made it possible for me to look at my own development as a strength rather than a collection of flaws.

- **Modifying Self-Talk and Permitting Positive Influences:**

This journey has been incredibly transforming in that it has allowed me to modify my self-talk intentionally. The stories we tell ourselves have so much power, and I have purposefully changed mine to be positive. In order to promote a more positive mental environment, affirmations, gratitude exercises, and mindful self-encouragement have become useful techniques. Surrounding yourself with good influences, whether from books, people, or events, has also been crucial in forming this newfound optimism.

- **Assessing and Modifying Relationships:**

The 50s were a time of reflection, which prompted a careful assessment of the relationships in my life. Some relationships have blossomed and developed, while others have needed to be adjusted or even let go of. Understanding how connections affect personal development has served as a compass for me, enabling me to give priority to those who advance my path.

- **The Magnificence of Being Wholly Oneself:**

The beauty of being really myself has maybe been the most freeing discovery. It has been a life-changing experience to let go of social expectations and embrace sincerity. It's about letting go of the need to fit in or be judged and embracing my actual self. My relationship with more and myself significantly others has improved as a result of my genuineness.

Navigating the Uncertainties

The world we used to know has changed, bringing with it a variety of difficulties that call for flexibility and fortitude. Understanding these difficulties acts as a compass for me, pointing the way through the unknown areas of this new world. Every problem is a chance for development and transformation, from adjustments to daily schedules to reassessing priorities.

Despite the challenges, I've discovered unanticipated sources of strength and development. The capacity to adjust to unanticipated events has emerged as a sign of human resilience. It's a voyage of self-discovery that reveals the resilience and hidden qualities that could have lain dormant in the absence of such obstacles.

Unquestionably, one of the unpredictable aspects of this journey has been personal loss. Embracing life's uncertainties requires acknowledging and processing these losses, whether they are of a loved one, a habit, or a feeling of normalcy. It's a process of figuring out how to appreciate the strength that results from such experiences while still managing the intricacies of loss.

Accepting life's uncertainties means actively interacting with life's ups and downs rather than obediently accepting your lot in life. It's a path that calls for striking a careful balance between accepting the inherent uncertainties of the human experience, accepting the trials, and finding strength in adversity.

- **Recognizing the Challenges and Adapting to a Changing World:**

Acknowledging the issues posed by the worldwide health crisis has been an essential first step on my path through them. I find myself standing at the nexus of uncertainty and adaptability as I face the changes in my surroundings, from the rearranged social relations to the reconfiguration of everyday routines. The familiar has changed in this setting, and realizing this has helped me on my expedition by providing a sense of direction.

Recalibrating expectations and having a flexible mentality are essential for adjusting to a changing reality. Though the terrain may seem foreign, I've been able to adjust my sails to the shifting winds by viewing the difficulties as learning opportunities. In the face of uncertainty, I am able to flourish because of my active participation in the world that is changing.

- **Finding Growth and Strength in the Face of Adversity:**

In the midst of the pandemic's challenges, I've discovered within myself unanticipated reserves of strength and progress. The experience of difficulty has turned into my personal growth, forcing me to uncover aspects of bravery and resilience that could have lain dormant in the absence of such hardships.

Finding strength and growth is a never-ending cycle of overcoming obstacles, changing with them, and growing stronger as a result. It entails making a deliberate effort to look for chances to grow and learn about oneself when facing hardship. I've turned trying times into stepping stones to a stronger, more capable version of myself by redefining obstacles as opportunities for personal development.

- **Acknowledging Personal Loss and Embracing Life's Uncertainties:**

The pandemic has not been without its fair share of human tragedies. Every loss needs to be acknowledged and processed, whether it is the severe loss of a loved one or the gradual breakdown of routine and normalcy. Acknowledging the unpredictability of life entails managing the intricacies of mourning while discovering methods to commemorate the fortitude that arises from such encounters.

Maintaining a careful equilibrium between lamenting the past and appreciating the present is necessary while dealing with personal loss. It is evidence of the ability of the human spirit to find meaning and purpose despite hardship. Recognizing that every event adds to a robust and adaptive existence, I've learned to traverse the unknown environment with a combination of fragility and strength by owning up to my personal losses.

Incorporating Quotes that Resonate with the Theme:

One such quote that has profoundly influenced my perspective is Eleanor Roosevelt's timeless words, "You gain strength, courage and confidence by every experience in which you really stop to look fear in the face. You are able to say to yourself, 'I have lived through this horror. I can take the next thing that comes along.' You must do the thing you think you cannot do." This quote summarizes the resilience and the transformative power inherent in confronting one's fears and challenges.

Another guiding principle in my journey comes from Rumi's poetic wisdom: "The wound is the place where the light enters you." Embracing the idea that challenges and wounds can be catalysts for growth and illumination has been a transformative shift in my mindset.

- **Sharing Personal Insights and Reflections:**

I've experienced epiphanies throughout my career and personal development, moments of deep knowledge that have influenced the way I see the world, myself, and other people. These epiphanies frequently result from reflective periods, talks with mentors, or the trial by fire of confronting and conquering obstacles.

Realizing that vulnerability is a source of tremendous power rather than a weakness has become a pillar of my philosophy of life. I've gained access to real relationships, self-discovery, and the ability to empathize with others by letting myself be vulnerable.

Throughout my life, contemplating the relationship between resilience and personal growth has also been essential. Realizing that obstacles are actually chances for progress, I've developed a mindset that looks for possibilities for reorientation and improvement in adversity and sees obstacles as stepping stones rather than obstacles.

My goal in sharing these personal thoughts is to provide glimpses into the complex mosaic of self-discovery rather than to impose a plan. Every realization adds up to the overall picture of empowerment and personal development.

Empowering Others: Inspiring Positive Change

A pillar of our conversations has been promoting introspection. The beauty of personal development is found in the ripple effects it has on the community as well as in the personal transformation of the individual. My goal with this platform is to inspire others by encouraging each listener to start their own journey of self-discovery and positive transformation.

It is crucial to keep going forward when faced with difficulties. Every incident serves as a reminder that we are capable of adapting, developing, and rising above difficulties. It's about accepting the possibility of constructive change and developing resilience in the face of adversity.

- **Encouraging Self-Reflection and Embracing Personal Growth:**

In my Podcast: Wide Open Spaces with Ilise, the primary goal has been to inspire self-reflection and personal improvement in each listener by encouraging them to go out on their own path. The capacity of introspection to foster positive development and provide avenues for self-awareness is what gives it its power. Accepting personal improvement is a journey toward being the best versions of ourselves, not merely a destination.

Highlighting the Importance of Moving Forward During Challenging Times:

Keeping going becomes crucial when faced with difficulties. Every episode reminds us that we have the ability to bounce back and develop despite the obstacles we face in life. It involves moving ahead of uncertainty while keeping an open mind and realizing that often, the most trying times lead to the most progress. Guiding us through the intricacies of life, the forward-thinking mentality serves as a light of strength and optimism.

Motivating Everyday Objectives for the Spirit, Body, and Mind:

It's not always only about getting things done; it's also about setting goals that support mental, physical, and spiritual health. Every daily objective becomes a step toward holistic development, ranging from cerebral activities to physical health maintenance and spiritual nourishment through practices like meditation.

Stressing the Need for Emotional Health and Self-Care:

Self-care is an essential component of emotional well-being, not merely a trendy term. Making self-care a priority and doing it on purpose has become a daily habit for me. Self-care, whether it takes the form of setting aside time for leisure, doing joyful activities, or just admitting and attending to emotional needs, is essential to living a robust and well-rounded life.

Practicing Mindfulness and Gratitude in Everyday Life:

Gratitude and mindfulness practices are daily affirmations that help me keep going. It helps me navigate moments of self-reflection. Practicing mindfulness or expressing thanks for the apparently ordinary things in life has shown the beauty that exists in every moment. It's about cultivating a mentality that improves general well-being, appreciating the good things in life, and living in the now. When integrated into daily life, gratitude and mindfulness become transforming skills for building a resilient and upbeat mentality.

Reflecting on the Transformative Power of Challenging Experiences:

Every challenge, every curve in the road, has sparked development, resiliency, and self-discovery. It's evidence of our extraordinary resilience that we not only survive but also come out of it smarter and stronger.

Encouraging Readers to Embrace the Journey to

Their Best Selves:

I really encourage everyone who has joined me on this quest to embrace the path to becoming your best self. It's a road characterized by introspection, deliberate development, and steadfast faith in the possibility of constructive change. May you find comfort in the idea that developing your greatest self is a continuous, ongoing process rather than a destination as we negotiate the complexity of life.

Exploring the Wide Open Spaces in One's World:

I'd like to end by asking you to take a moment to reflect on the vast open spaces in your life. These areas are not simply the geographical landscapes; they are also the uncharted territories, the potential that lies just beneath the surface of our being. Above all, enjoy the beauty of being really yourself. Accept change and rise to difficulties. The journey of life is one of continuous discovery, and in these broad open spaces, you have the chance to develop, have joy, and reach your greatest potential.

Chapter 11 – The Quest Within

Explore Your Own Paths and Aspirations

Every individual is a traveler down the wandering path of life, moving through the valleys of doubt and ascending the heights of achievement. We find the essence of who we really are and the limitless potential that lies inside us within the folds of this journey.

We learn the profound insight that results from self-discovery and personal development in the quiet times of contemplation. It's a journey filled with both victories and setbacks, and every one of them helps to mold us into the people we were always intended to be. By using self-awareness as a lens, we may see our purpose and direction clearly, shedding new light on the way forward.

I invite you all to boldly and cautiously welcome the new chapters of your own story as they emerge. Go into the unexplored areas of your desires and aspirations since it is in pursuing these goals that we discover the real meaning of happiness and satisfaction. Your journey is a one-of-a-kind artwork that is just waiting to be revealed, woven together with the threads of your experiences, goals, and desires.

As we explore the depths of our own self-discovery, let's honor the transforming potential that every one of us possesses. It is a voyage of great significance, one that goes beyond place and temporal constraints and leads us to a better knowledge of both the world and ourselves.

Understanding Roadblocks

I.   Exploring The Concept of Roadblocks in Life's Journey

We all face obstacles on our path to self-awareness and personal development, which put our commitment to the test and our resilience to the test. These weaknesses—both material and immaterial—act as strong roadblocks in the way of our goals, forcing us to make our way through the difficulties and uncertainties of life.

As we go more into the idea of obstacles, we see that they take many different shapes, each with unique difficulties and barriers to get beyond. Physical restrictions, financial hardships, or logistical issues are examples of real impediments that limit efficiency and progress. Conversely, intangible obstacles might be limited beliefs, self-doubt, or a fear of failing, which prevents us from reaching our full potential and pursuing our goals with confidence and conviction.

II.   Tangible and Intangible Roadblocks

These roadblocks, which differ in kind and source, can be generally divided into concrete and intangible barriers, each of which poses a different set of difficulties for us as we strive for happiness and achievement.

A variety of tangible and intangible roadblocks can act as tangible obstacles, making it more difficult for us to proceed along the path of our choice. These might be economic limitations, administrative difficulties, or rational roadblocks that restrict our choices and delay our progress. For example, a lack of funds or unstable finances may make it difficult for us to seek higher education or make professional changes, and practical issues like transportation or access to necessary services may make it difficult for us to accomplish our objectives.

Conversely, intangible roadblocks take the shape of interpersonal, psychological, and emotional challenges that weaken our resilience, self-assurance, and fortitude. These might include limiting beliefs that limit our potential and prevent us from taking chances and seizing new possibilities, as well as self-doubt, perfectionism, fear of failing, and fear of success. Furthermore, our well-being can be negatively impacted by interpersonal disputes, toxic relationships, and unfavorable settings, which can undermine our self-worth and demotivate us from pursuing our goals.

You must confront your challenges head-on, strengthen your resilience, deepen your self-awareness, and emerge stronger and more empowered on the other side.

It is impossible to overestimate the influence of obstacles on well-being and personal development. Whether they are material or immaterial, difficulties put our commitment and resilience to the test. These kinds of challenges are common on our trip. These obstacles have the capacity to sabotage our sense of direction, erode our self-assurance, and elicit emotions of annoyance, disappointment, and hopelessness.

They can also hinder our capacity to advance, limit our creativity, and realize our dreams and ambitions. Roadblocks may worsen tension, worry, and feelings of inadequacy if they are not addressed, which, over time, can damage our mental and emotional health. Roadblocks, as disruptive as they may be, can also present worthwhile chances for development, education, and self-discovery. We become more resilient, adaptive, and resourceful when we overcome adversity, which improves our ability to solve problems and increases our self-awareness.

Furthermore, conquering challenges gives us a stronger feeling of self-efficacy, confidence, and a deep sense of empowerment and success. In the end, we develop the resilience and inner fortitude required to prosper in the face of life's unavoidable challenges by facing and overcoming our obstacles.

Coping with Stress and Uncertainty

Our ability to handle stress and uncertainty becomes critical to our resilience and overall well-being. We frequently find ourselves struggling with excessive expectations, unforeseen difficulties, and the constant weight of uncertainty. In the middle of this, developing strong coping strategies becomes crucial to our capacity to ride out the ups and downs of life.

First and foremost, we must acknowledge the importance of coping strategies in our day-to-day existence. These systems are extremely useful for controlling stress emotional responses and regaining internal equilibrium in the chaos of contemporary life. Adopting coping mechanisms gives us the ability to face hardship with bravery, resiliency, and grace; this promotes a feeling of empowerment and self-control in the face of life's many obstacles.

I.   Personal Shield: The Coping Strategy

The idea of the "personal shield" is a potent metaphor for the safeguards we might put in place to ensure our mental and emotional health in the face of life's obstacles. Similar to the armor used by brave fighters, the personal shield serves as a metaphorical wall that protects us against the barrage of outside pressures and detrimental effects.

There are several ways to visualize the personal shield, each suited to your own requirements and preferences. Some of you may experience it as a warm, comforting light that seems to be emanating from the inside and covers our inner landscape with a sense of peace and calmness. This vision envelops us in a cocoon of emotional resilience and self-assurance, bringing emotions of warmth, security, and tranquility.

Furthermore, the personal shield fosters a feeling of empowerment and authority by acting as a constant reminder that we have the ability to create the reality we want and overcome obstacles in life with grace and resiliency. It gives us a strong sense of self-confidence and independence, enabling us to face hardship with poise and assurance.

II.   Implementing Self-care Practices

Let's now discuss practical methods for implementing self-care into your everyday routine. Mindfulness meditation is one of my favorite meditation techniques. It has been incredibly transforming to set aside even a little period of time every day for introspection. I may develop present-moment awareness and find serenity in the chaos of everyday life with its assistance.

In my self-care toolbox, deep breathing exercises are another indispensable resource. I use deep breathing to center myself and regain my composure whenever I feel stress or tension rising. It's incredible how even something as basic as paying attention to your breathing can have such a significant effect on your well-being.

And nature is another. Yes, nature has this amazing power to restore spiritual energy. Spending time outside, whether it be for a quiet stroll in the park or a strenuous climb in the mountains, helps me rediscover the peace and beauty of the natural world. It feels as though my stress levels have been reset.

Of course, a major part of my self-care regimen also involves creativity. Whether I'm writing, drawing, or performing music, creative expression gives me a healthy and useful method to communicate my feelings. For me, it serves as a type of therapy, allowing me to explore my emotions and ideas while having fun.

And lastly, some calm reflection. I may connect with my inner knowledge and find clarity in the midst of turmoil by setting aside time to journal, practice meditation, or just be with my thoughts. I find my center in these quiet times when I can really pay attention to what my body and mind require.

I've learned to refuel my inner supplies of strength and resilience by making self-care a priority. They have become my compass, bringing me back to equilibrium and well-being when I'm feeling anxious or stressed. Even if practicing self-care is a journey, it is always worthwhile. Never forget that you should give your mental and emotional well-being first priority. You are worthy of success.

Exploring Inner Strength

- ## Significance of Inner Strength and Resilience

Exploring inner power feels similar to setting out on a very intimate journey into what we are. It's about revealing the layers of resilience that are just waiting to be found and welcomed within each of us. Examining the importance of inner strength has been nothing short of transformational for me.

I've discovered that resilience—the capacity to rise above misfortune—is what true inner strength is all about, not merely pushing through difficulties. It is finding the bravery to face our doubts and anxieties head-on with the knowledge that we are capable of overcoming them.

I've faced numerous challenges and disappointments on my own path, each of which has tried my patience. However, it's at those terrible times that I've realized the full extent of my inner power. I've discovered strength and resiliency in myself that I never had an idea I had in the face of hardship.

And I've learned the value of inner strength from more than simply my personal experiences. The tales of fortitude that others have shared with me have greatly motivated me; their victories over apparently insurmountable obstacles and their unflinching will to endure hardship.

I'm passionate about enabling others to access their inner reserves of bravery and fortitude because of this. Every single one of us, in my opinion, has an inner strength that can get us through even the worst of circumstances. It's about accepting our weaknesses and turning them into opportunities for further growth and resilience.

I want you, my readers, to know that you are far stronger than you think. You possess the ability to rise above any difficulty and surpass every barrier that you face. There will surely be times of uncertainty and doubt, and it might not always be simple. However, have faith in your inner strength since it is a formidable power.

Nurturing The Self

My dear friends, nurturing oneself is a path of kindness and self-discovery that I have personally taken. It's about realizing how important it is to take care of our mental health and putting our needs first, even in the face of life's responsibilities.

I now understand that taking care of ourselves is not selfish; rather, it is necessary for our general well-being. We must take care of our own hearts and minds in the same way that we tend to the needs of others. It's about recognizing our deservingness of love and care despite what those around us would attempt to tell us differently.

- **Prioritize Self-Care and Introspection**

I've learned it hard way that no matter how crucial it is to set aside time for reflection and self-care, even in the middle of stress. These tiny actions of self-nurturing, like going for a leisurely walk in the outdoors, engaging in a favorite pastime, or just taking some time to think about the day's events, have been crucial in helping me to keep my emotional balance.

I urge you to put reflection and self-care first in your own life. Spend some time tending to your heart and soul's needs, honoring your feelings, and listening to your inner voice. It's about tending to the flame of self-love and compassion that burns within each of us, about finding fulfillment and balance in the midst of life's chaos.

Self-care is essential; it's not a luxury. We may develop a strong inner resilience and strength that gets us through life's ups and downs by practicing self-compassion and kindness. Have faith in the life-changing potential of self-care, and understand that by taking care of yourself, you are sowing the seeds of contentment, happiness, and serenity in your own life.

Embracing Possibilities

My dear friends, as our journey draws to a close, I find myself thinking about the transformational potential of self-discovery. We've experienced highs and lows, periods of clarity and uncertainty, but despite it all, we've developed and matured in ways we never would have imagined.

I want to exhort each and every one of you to bravely and optimistically embrace the vast open spaces in life. Life is full of opportunities just waiting to be discovered and pursued. It is our responsibility to take fearless risks, welcome change with open arms, and have faith in the path ahead.

I am very appreciative of the chance to interact with each of you and share these ideas. It has been an honor to accompany you on this path of self-awareness and development. I cannot adequately convey how much your presence and your willingness to go into the depths of your own souls have inspired me.

Recall that the process of self-discovery is continuous. It's a trip that gets better every day with every new encounter and chance to develop. So, bravely, my dear friends, embrace the opportunities that lie ahead of you. And all the best!

Conclusion

Greetings, my lovely readers,

As our journey together draws to a close, I want to take a moment to express my heartfelt gratitude to you for joining me on this exploration of personal development. Thank you for entrusting me with your time and attention and for allowing me to be a part of your quest for growth and self-discovery. It has been an honor and a privilege to accompany you on this journey, to witness your dedication to personal transformation, and to share in the joys and challenges along the way.

As we near the end of our journey, let's consider the important lessons and deep insights we have discussed. I really hope that every chapter would have acted as a stepping stone, assisting us as we navigate personal growth and self-discovery. We have traveled through a terrain full of insight and development, from accepting life's uncertainties to exploring the limits of inner power.

Remember how we first struggled with the idea of reinvention? We discussed how development and change are inevitable, acknowledging that our goals and identities are dynamic. We discovered hidden goals and objectives via introspection and contemplation, which laid the foundation for our transformational path.

And now, at the end of our journey, here we are, poised to experience more personal development and progress. We've had difficulties and obstacles along the way, as well as periods of doubt and uncertainty. But every challenge we've faced has made us stronger and more resilient than before.

Take as much time as required to reflect on your own development. Examine your current self in comparison to the person you were when we started this adventure together. Take note of the small changes in your perspective, the fresh focus on your objectives, and the expanded self-awareness.

Take On Obstacles With Bravery and Hope

We face innumerable difficulties and barriers on our path through life, some of which may appear insurmountable. However, it is at these times of difficulty that our genuine fortitude and resiliency become evident. I want to inspire you to approach every obstacle with courage and everlasting optimism. Have faith in your capacity to conquer any challenges that may arise. Never forget that every setback presents a chance for development and education. With an optimistic outlook and the knowledge that you possess the inner fortitude to endure, take on every problem head-on.

Resilience In Handling The Ups And Downs Of Life

There are many unforeseen diversions and turns in life that might leave us feeling disoriented and insecure. Resilience becomes our most valuable ally at these times. The capacity to overcome obstacles, adjust, and flourish in the face of adversity is resilience. By strengthening your inner fortitude and reaching out to your support system, you may develop resilience. Bring in the good energy around you and remember how you overcame obstacles in the past. Recognize that you possess the fortitude to overcome whatever challenge life presents.

Throughout our time together, I have had the privilege of sharing reflections, experiences, and insights with you, for which I am really thankful. My life has been profoundly enhanced by the relationships we've built, the discussions we've had, and the epiphanies we've had together.

I appreciate your willingness to participate in in-depth reflection and discussion, as well as your openness and sensitivity. We have created a community of empowerment and progress by sharing our experiences and encouraging one another to embrace life's limitless potential and set new goals.

Encouraging Ongoing Self-Reflection and Growth

Always remember that the journey of self-discovery does not end here. It is, in fact, a continuous process that calls for constant introspection and development. I urge you to continue asking yourself the difficult questions about who you are and who you want to be and to keep the channels of reflection open. Accept the benefit of writing your ideas and experiences; it can be a very useful tool for introspection and personal growth. Every entry is a window into your changing identity, serving as a remembrance of your past as well as a roadmap for your future.

Additionally, look for fresh opportunities to push yourself beyond your comfort zone. You're committing to a lifetime of personal development when you take advantage of these possibilities for growth, which frequently occur in the places where you feel least comfortable.

Resources For Further Exploration And Support

I want to leave you with some tools that can be used as guides to help you on your never-ending adventure. Consider establishing connections with online communities and forums devoted to self-improvement and self-care. Along with encouragement and support, you'll find a variety of viewpoints that can further your own development and knowledge here.

I also suggest reading books and taking part in workshops that go further into the topics we've covered. These resources may provide you with new perspectives and useful guidance to assist you in navigating the challenges of your own path, whether you're looking to learn more about self-care, resilience, or mindfulness.

The path to personal growth is enduring and never-ending. It calls us to not only travel wisely but also to stop, think, and take in the surroundings as we go. Every stride and every fall has a lesson that is specific to everyone of us to learn. Remember that personal development is an ongoing process rather than a destination as you proceed.

My sincere goal for every one of you is that you continue to find happiness and fulfillment in your quest for self-care and personal development as we formally part ways. I hope you always treat yourself with kindness, especially when it feels like progress is eluding you. Never forget that there are new opportunities every day to take care of your body, mind, and soul.

Continue your exploration, dreaming, and, most importantly, your growth. The ability to meet challenges head-on, bounce back from setbacks with grace, and recognize your own worth at every turn are qualities that greatly enhance the road of personal growth.

Thank you for allowing me to be a part of your story. Here's to your success and happiness, today and always.

With warmth and best wishes,

Ilise